Social-Emotional Learning (SEL) in the Home

A Practical Guide for Integrating the Development of Social-Emotional Skills into Your Parenting

William B. Ribas, Ph.D.

Deborah A. Brady, Ph.D.

Jane M. Hardin, M.Ed.

Elayne Gumlaw, M.Ed.

RIBAS ASSOCIATES AND PUBLICATIONS, INC.

Published and distributed by Ribas Publications
596 Pleasant Street
Norwood, MA 02062
Website: ribasassociates.com
Phone: 781-551-9120

ISBN: 978-0-99-761091-8

Book design and typesetting by Jane Tenenbaum
Graphic on front cover reprinted with permission from CASEL.org

Printed in Canada

DEDICATIONS

To my children and grandchildren, the source of my greatest consternation, perplexity, enlightenment, and joy.—Deborah Brady

To my parents, husband and children who loved and supported me every step of the way and to the next generation who will continue the journey for me.—Elayne Gumlaw

For all those who love and care for children.—Jane Hardin

For my children Anna and Will, with all my love.—Bill Ribas

CONTENTS

3   Resolving Conflicts and Other Important Conversations with Your Child   71

4   How Questions Encourage Higher-Order Thinking and Deep Conversations about Social-Emotional Skills   113

5   The Brain and Learning   149

Index   199

INTRODUCTION

If you are buying this book because

1. you think the authors want to (or are able to) tell you how to parent your child, or,
2. you think the authors believe they are better parents/guardians than you,

put it back on the shelf and save your money!

No one can really tell you how to better parent your child unless they have a comprehensive understanding of you, of how you parent, and of your child. We authors are not experts on parenting. We are experts on the development of social-emotional skills in young people.

Just to prove the point that I am not an exemplar parent, I will tell you about a conversation I had recently with my son, who is in college and had an emergency root canal. Later that day I called him to ask him how bad it was (I never had a root canal). His answer was, "Dad, nothing could be as bad as that time you made me skate through a two-hour hockey practice with double pneumonia when I was 11!"

In my own defense, I didn't know he had double pneumonia until we took him to the doctor the next day. In hindsight, I guess I should have known something was up when he came home from school and slept until practice time and I all but carried him into the car for practice. The worst part of this is that I have more stories like this about my parenting mess ups!

I like to think that my kids are doing well in part *because of* my parenting. The reality is that they might be doing well *in spite of* my parenting!

—Bill Ribas

Authors' Expertise

The area in which we do have expertise is in developing social and emotional skills (SEL skills) in young people, which they can use in school and life. Our knowledge has come from hundreds of hours working with teachers and children many hours studying the research, books, and articles on SEL. As you will learn in the book, our "intelligence" related to this topic is due to study and practice. It is not due to our being smarter or better parents than any of our readers.

We authors are all parents, and this experience has been invaluable. We learned from our successes and our failures. Doing the research on social-emotional learning (SEL)—specifically for this book—allowed us to reflect on our own past parenting and to think about our present and future parenting with our own children.

What Is in This Book?

In writing this book, we planned to provide parents with a set of strategies that could easily be integrated into their parenting everyday. As mentioned above, we are not telling you how to parent. Rather, we are helping you meld your successful parenting practices with strategies that will help you to further develop your child's social-emotional learning.

In chapter 1 you will learn about the significant positive impacts on the lives of children, adolescents, and young adults when they have learned SEL skills. This research has motivated schools across the country to train teachers, administrators, and other school staff in the skills for developing social-emotional learning. With this book, parents can now be significant contributors to this important work. During a child's pre-school to high school experience, the school teaches 95% of the academic skills (reading, writing, math, science). As parents, we may provide some support for academics by helping with homework and reading to our children. However, with SEL skills, parents and guardians *can contribute 50% or more* to the skill development because every parenting activity is an opportunity to develop these skills. We have the opportunity to impact the development of SEL skills from birth through the rest of their lives.

We hope that while reading this book you will find new ways to positively affect your children's lives. The book provides strategies, tools, and examples to make this important work more effective and fulfilling.

Below is a brief summary of what you will learn in each chapter.

Chapter 1: What Is Social-Emotional Learning?

After reading this chapter, parents and guardians will be able to:

1. Explain the five major areas of SEL skills
2. Explain the specific social and emotional skills related to each of the five areas
3. Explain the impact on children and adolescents in school, work, and life when SEL skills are learned
4. Explain the stages children and adolescents follow from initial exposure to a skill to its mastery

Chapter 2: Beliefs about Intelligence and the Acquisition of Academic, Social, and Emotional Skills

After reading this chapter, parents and guardians will be able to:

1. Explain how to help your children (of all ages) confront and overcome challenging tasks
2. Explain the role of genetics and learned skills as they relate to school, work, and life success
3. Explain the SEL skills possessed by successful people and how to help your children develop these skills

Chapter 3: Resolving Conflicts and Other Important Conversations with Your Child

After reading this chapter, parents and guardians will be able to:

1. Plan ahead for important discussions with your child to insure you achieve the goals of the conversation
2. Use effective praise to maximize your child's acquisition of SEL skills
3. Use descriptive feedback to maximize your child's acquisition of SEL skills
4. Explain the difference between punishments and consequences and use consequences effectively
5. Take important conversations with your child through stages to maximize your child's acquisition of SEL skills
6. Facilitate the resolution of conflicts between your child and friends and between siblings by modeling skills they can use to resolve future conflicts

Chapter 4: How Questions Encourage Higher-Order Thinking and Deep Conversations about Social-Emotional Skills

After reading this chapter, parents and guardians will be able to:

1. Explain how to have the five essential social-emotional conversations with your child as he or she grows to adulthood:
   a. Who are you?
   b. How do your actions reflect who you are?
   c. How do you read social signals from others?
   d. How to get along with friends and family?
   e. How to make decisions that reflect your values?

2. Explain how to encourage children to engage in meaningful conversations about the important parts of their lives: themselves, their behavior, their relationships, their choices

3. Explain how to create a supportive "safe space" for meaningful conversations that support children's social-emotional growth at all ages.

4. Explain how to establish trusting relationships that are at the core of all deep conversations

5. Explain how to support the development of higher-order thinking and metacognition through conversations using books, movies, and activities to evoke and support those conversations

Chapter 5: The Brain and Learning

After reading this chapter, parents and guardians will be able to:

1. Explain the basics of brain anatomy and how the brain functions

2. Explain the processes of memory creation and learning and how they are connected

3. Explain how the brain functions in relation to learning social and emotional skills

4. Distinguish between common "neuro" myths and research-backed findings about the brain

5. Use knowledge of learning and memory processes to optimize experiences in the reader's parenting practices

As you read this book, it is important that you take time to acknowledge the good work you already do as a parent. In fact, as you read Chapter 1, you will see that you are already developing many of these skills in your children. You may not have used the same name for the skill or have thought that the interactions were "teaching" them. However, we are confident you will recognize how parenting actions you took, and the modelling you provided, did, in fact, positively impact your child's SEL skills level.

Our hope is that this book will help you take the next step in this important process.

Using *Social-Emotional Learning (SEL) in the Home* in Your Book Study Group

Like our children, we all have different learning styles. Our learning style is the way in which we are most successful at learning new information and skills. For some of us, just reading this book and working with our child is the way we can best assist with the development of SEL skills. For others, meeting weekly or monthly in a book discussion group is effective. We wrote this book so parents can work individually with their child or participate in a parent book group.

For those who prefer working in a book group we have written the book so it can be easily used by groups with no training. Each chapter has discussion questions the group can use as they progress through the book. Some book groups may wish to discuss each chapter separately. Others may wish to study it in other ways (e.g., skill by skill). To assist parents with this, we have developed two book-group protocols that will make it easy for groups of two, three, four, or more (we recommend groups not exceed eight members) to learn together. We don't mean to imply these are the only two ways this book can be used in a group. Parent book groups should feel free to use the book in any way that best meet their needs. On the following pages, we offer these two protocols as a way to easily approach the book if your group believes it best meets their needs.

Option 1: Chapter-by-Chapter Format

Book study groups are a way for parents/guardians to work with one another to better parent their child(ren). When running a book group it is important to have a well-established structure for the group to be productive for all. The following guidelines for a chapter-by-chapter book study group is intended to assist parents with having productive book study groups.

1. **Groups should have between two to eight members.** When the group exceeds eight it reduces the opportunities for each member to speak.

2. **Groups can meet weekly, every two weeks, or every three weeks.** If meeting weekly, it is important that reading "assignments" are short enough so everyone can complete the reading. When book groups meet less frequently than every three weeks, too much information from the previous meeting is forgotten and it can be difficult to pick up the discussion where you left off.

3. **Groups can be established in many configurations.** For example, they can be made up of the parents/guardians of children of a similar age or they can be made up of parents/guardians of children of multiple ages.

4. **Group Leaders:** It is important to have some form of leadership to keep the discussion on track. Any of the following have been used successfully.

    a. **Groups with a permanent leader and assistant leader.** The leader keeps the discussion moving and insures equitable sharing. The assistant keeps notes of key points and keeps track of the time. The leader and the assistant remain the same through all the meetings.

    b. **Groups with permanent co-leaders.** In situations in which there are co-leaders the leaders can alternate sessions. When one is the leader and the other is the assistant leader. The co-leaders remain the same through all the meetings.

    c. **Alternating leaders and assistant leaders.** The roles of leader and assistant leader can alternate each session or every couple of sessions. In some cases there may be parents who are uncomfortable acting as a leader or co-leader. In those situations the leadership should only be alternated among those who are willing to take a leadership role. Since it is important to get as many people involved in book groups as possible, we don't want anyone to be deterred from participating if he or she is reticent to take a leadership role.

5. **At the first meeting, establish norms for productive discussion and have the group commit to following these norms.** At the outset of each session, ask everyone to do a quick skim of the norms as a good reminder. This may not be necessary if the group meets every week. In this case, reviewing the norms at the first two sessions, and then as needed, may be sufficient. Below is a sample of norms that can be used. However, each group should feel free to modify these suggested norms to best meet the group's needs.

   a. I did my reading prior to the group meeting.

   b. I understand that good parenting can come in many forms. I did not try to impose my parenting belief and practices on others.

   c. I shared my ideas and offered suggestions *when suggestions were requested* while insuring others had equal time to share.

   d. I spoke clearly and slowly.

   e. I answered others' questions but did not monopolize the discussion.

   f. I remained on topic and helped the group stay focused.

   g. I encouraged others to participate and respected their contributions.

   h. When I disagreed, I did so without hurting others' feelings.

   i. I summarized or repeated my ideas when necessary.

   j. I gave reasons for my opinions.

   k. I listened courteously and effectively.

   l. I tried to understand the suggestions of others when those suggestions were not consistent with my own ideas and beliefs.

6. **The reading should be broken into defined sections that can be discussed at a single meeting.** Books typically need to be broken up into chapters or sections. Our book has five chapters that are concise and defined. Some study groups do one chapter at a meet-

ing. Some will take two or three meetings to discuss a chapter. Some groups will divide the chapters among the groups and have each chapter group report on the chapter during a meeting.

7. **All members of the group should complete the reading prior to the next meeting.** Discuss the importance of doing the reading so the group will run well. Not reading impacts everyone (not just the person who didn't read).

8. **The type of analysis and some focus questions should be agreed upon prior to completing the reading.** This book contains focus questions at the end of each chapter. The group may use these questions or create their own. The focus questions should be reviewed prior to the reading of each section. The questions then become the focus of discussion at the next session.

9. **The most interesting pieces to discuss tend to be those that enable parents/guardians to immediately apply the concepts in the reading to their children.** This book has been written by four parents. Each chapter is filled with strategies that are immediately applicable and easy to implement.

10. **Action Step** (optional): Once the group has mastered the content in a particular reading, it is time to add a practical experience. Each person should identify one or more strategies in the reading with which to experiment at home. We say "experiment" because the strategy might succeed—or it might fail. As scientists know, however, you often learn more from failures then you do from successes. After experimenting with the strategy, the member should prepare a reflection with answers to the following questions:
    a. Why did I choose this strategy?
    b. What worked? Why did it work?
    c. What did not work? Why didn't it work?
    d. If I try this strategy again, what will I do differently?

The reflection is shared and discussed at the next group meeting. If a group chooses to use this optional step, only members who volunteer should be selected to share. It should be made clear to all that no one is required to share. Some people wish to learn just by listening. They should have the option to do so without the pressure of needing to share.

Option 2: A Timed Protocol for Larger Groups

The timed protocol provides structure and allots a specific amount of time summarizing, sharing, and discussing. The protocol guarantees that all group members have an opportunity to share their thoughts about what they've read and how they can connect it to their parenting. If your group is large, the following process provides a structure.

The protocol asks parents to select and share passages of the book that resonate and "jump out at them." This structure gives every participant a chance to connect their own experiences with the book.

The protocol provides everyone an equal voice and time. The timing helps organize the sharing and prevents one issue or one person from sidetracking or taking over the discussion.

A time-keeper assures that the talking time ("air time") for each person is protected and guaranteed.

Finally, the protocol helps the group reach their desired destination—sharing and discussing social and emotional experiences and practices in childhood and adolescence.

Please note that the timing is for an hour. These times can be adjusted to the allotted time, the size of the group, and other needs of the group.

Preparation Before the First Meeting

1. Decide on whether to discuss the whole book in one evening or to meet more frequently to discuss one chapter at a time.

2. Ask the participants to read the book (or chapter) with an eye for passages that "speak to them" because they connect with their own parental concerns or with concerns for their children. Ask the group members to mark one or two passages per chapter and to write their reaction on a post-it or note card. A sample is in the box below with the quote and the connection to their concerns.

3. Then ask the participants to add a question to each selected passage. The question is intended to invite others into the conversation.

Sample Post-it or Note Card

The Passage *(it can simply be circled in the book and not copied)*:

Clinical psychologist Daniel Goleman, Ph.D., author of numerous books and articles on emotional intelligence, estimates that IQ only accounts for between 10 percent and 20 percent of a person's success in school and career.

My reaction or connection:

I was amazed by the fact that so little of a person's success is tied to the intelligence they are born with. It is almost **scary how much impact parents and teachers can have on children's success**.

Question:

What is an example of something you have done with your child to help him or her develop one of the SEL skills?

Timing the Meeting

The protocol below is like a meeting agenda and helps you plan the meeting and the results that you anticipate. You can share the protocol with participants before the first meeting.

The times in parentheses below can be changed to fit the time available. In the **Sample Book Club Protocol** below, the time is enough to discuss one chapter.

Step 1. Provides an overview of the chapter. The chapter objectives and the questions at the end of the chapter can provide a guide for the facilitator. You could ask for volunteers for the facilitation of each chapter.

Step 2. Provides time for discussion in small groups, so everyone has an opportunity to share their selected passages and concerns. Each person has 4–5 minutes and the facilitator (or timekeeper) keeps track of the time and makes sure everyone has adequate time to speak.

Step 3. Provides time for whole-group sharing. A member from each group summarizes the major question(s) for 2 minutes, followed by questions and comments from the group for about 3 minutes.

Step 4. Can vary. If members have tried some of the suggestions in the book, they can share their experiences. Or, to connect the meeting to the group's shared concerns, the facilitator may pose a question to the entire group.

Step 5. For planning the next meeting and next steps of the group or book club. Parents may decide to focus on one small area to share with the group at the next meeting.

Sample Book Club Protocol/Agenda (45–50 minutes)

1. **(5 minutes)** The facilitator summarizes the essence of the chapter.
2. **(20–25 minutes)** The facilitator asks the parents and guardians to share their selected passages in small groups of 4 or 5, allotting each person 4 or 5 minutes.
3. **(10–15 minutes)** Each group is asked to select a spokesperson who discusses the group's comments and passages for 5 minutes. Other groups can ask questions.
4. **(15 minutes)** The last part is variable. The facilitator may be aware of a current concern of the group, or may present an activity, article, video, or question to engage the entire group.
5. **(5 minutes)** At the end of each session, participants might consider a really small topic, or practice that they can research or try in their parenting, which they can share at the next meeting.

What Is Social-Emotional Learning?

The social-emotional learning (SEL) movement is a thoughtfully created structure for organizing what effective parents and guardians have done instinctively for decades. This structure organizes the development of intrapersonal and interpersonal learning and skills as follows: Intrapersonal skills are those that we use to understand our own behavior, emotions, and beliefs, while interpersonal skills are those that we use when interacting with others.

Credit must go to the Collaborative for Academic, Social, and Emotional Learning (CASEL), the Yale University Center for Emotional Intelligence, and other groups that have been working to promote the value of social-emotional learning for many years. CASEL eventually coalesced these ideas into the SEL movement based on the positive impact of these skills. Later in the chapter, we will share with you the positive impact of SEL on people's academic, emotional, social, and work lives.

Based on the analysis of more than two hundred social-emotional learning programs in schools, the academic performance of students who participated in these programs improved 11 percent (Durlak et al., 2017). Although these programs varied widely, Durlak and others discovered the following positive results in the school setting.

A Safe, Caring Environment in School Improves Students' Social-Emotional Skills

- If students have adequate SEL skills to work with others, their participation in collaborative and group learning situations increases their achievement and engagement.

- When teachers are trained in pro-social skills, high-risk behaviors among students working with their peers are decreased and their attitude toward school becomes more positive.

In this book, we are going to take this learning and translate it into the interactions between parents and children/adolescents in the home and the impact of parenting that develops social-emotional learning in children. However, as you will see below, the skills are the same, whether developed by the actions of teachers, counselors, or parents. This book looks at the ways in which these skills can be developed by parents or guardians by adjusting their daily parenting practices to develop these skills in their children.

CASEL categorized these skills into five major areas (CASEL, 2016) and developed a structure to promote the development of SEL skills in schools, homes, and community programs, as shown in Figure 1.1.

In Tables 1.1 to 1.5, we describe each of the five major SEL areas, along with their corresponding skills for parents and children in the home. The definition of each area and the first column in the tables are based on CASEL's work (http://www.casel.org/core-competencies/). The second column is based on work found in a 2014 article by Nicholas Yoder. We have adapted the tables by adding specificity and making them more user-friendly for parents and guardians. After each table, we have included real vignettes shared by parents, which represent either the child's or the parent's behavior or how they demonstrate some or all of the skills.

Figure 1.1 Social and Emotional Learning

As you become more familiar with the skills described in these tables, you will see that the five areas are often interdependent. For example, after Table 1.4, Relationship Management, we have provided a tool for developing social awareness. Children or adolescents use the tool to increase their awareness of how they work as part of a "team."

The skills of teamwork that are assessed in the table are also found in Table 1.5, Responsible Decision-Making.

Know Thyself

Tables 1.1–1.5 are also designed to help you help your child develop social and emotional skills. However, you will be much more effective at helping your child if you spend some time evaluating and improv-

You will be much more effective at helping your child if you spend time evaluating and improving your own skills in these areas.

ing *your own* skills in these areas for the following two reasons. First, **evaluating your own skills will give you a better idea of how you can develop the skills in your child.** Second, **your children will learn as much from what they see you do as from what they hear you say.** In Chapter 2, we talk more about conscious and unconscious beliefs and how they impact our own SEL skills and behaviors, as well as those of our children.

Five Areas of Social-Emotional Learning

Self-Awareness

Self-awareness is the ability to accurately recognize one's own emotions, thoughts, and values, and how they influence behavior. This is the ability to accurately assess one's strengths and limitations with a well-grounded sense of confidence and optimism when addressing new and difficult tasks." Table 1.1 lists specific self-awareness behaviors in the left column. The right column lists behaviors that children, adolescents, and adults exhibit when they master these skills.

Table 1.1 Self-Awareness Connected to Parenting Practices

Self-Awareness	Skills Related to the Competencies
• Identifying emotions • Accurate self-perception • Recognizing strengths • Self-confidence • Self-efficacy • Goal Setting	• Label and recognize your own and others' emotions. • Recognize your thinking strategies (a.k.a. metacognition). • Identify what triggers your own emotions. • Accurately recognize your own strengths and limitations. • Identify your own needs and values. • Possess self-efficacy and self-esteem. • Be able to apply a growth mindset to difficult tasks.

Parenting Example

The summer before my son entered college, he worked for me on tasks in my office. His work area was just through a doorway and it was easy for me to see what he was doing. I noticed that when confronted by some tasks he found difficult, he would "shut down" shortly after attempting the task. Despite my having told him to come to me when he was stuck, he would sit and be frustrated for long periods of time. Having had many years of seeing him do homework, and at times helping him, I knew that when frustrated he would shut down and make no further effort to overcome the challenge.

When I saw this behavior at work, I would go in and ask him, "How are you doing?" and then help him over the hurdle. I began to think about him being at college in the fall, with no parent there to help him when he got frustrated. I decided to change my tactic since neither I, nor anyone else, would be there to intervene and offer immediate assistance. The next time I saw him stopped with frustration, I sat with him and said, "I noticed that when you get frustrated you stop working. Rather than asking for help, you sit for long periods of time being "stuck." I'd like you to try something. If you are working on something and you are having trouble completing it, check how long you have been trying. If it is more than 10 minutes, ask me for help. If I am not available, go on to something else until you can get help." I then helped him solve the problem.

I needed to repeat this conversation over the course of a couple of weeks before he finally would use the skill as we had discussed. At times, I would see him forget to ask for help, but gradually his self-monitoring improved.

It wasn't until October that I learned that our little "experiment" had indeed caused a change in his self-awareness. I was talking with him on the phone about his college classes and he said to me, "I have been noticing that when I get stuck, I do what you said I do. I shut down. I have been catching myself. When it happens, I do something else and then go to the extra help lab."

Despite working with him all summer, I had no idea if the strategy I used with him during the summer had any lasting effect. It was only through that conversation, other school year conversations, and his academic success his freshman year in college that I knew there had been a change. It taught me that it is never too late to help our children develop these skills.

Self-Management

Self-management is the ability to successfully regulate one's emotions, thoughts, and behaviors in different situations—effectively managing stress, controlling impulses, and motivating oneself. This includes the ability to set and work toward personal, academic, and work goals. Table 1.2 lists specific self-management behaviors in the left column and the behaviors people demonstrate when they master these skills on the right.

Table 1.2 Self-Management Connected to Parenting Practices

Self-Management	Skills Related to the Competencies
• Set plans and work toward goals. • Overcome obstacles and create strategies for addressing longer-term goals. • Seek help when needed. • Manage personal and interpersonal stress.	• Set plans to achieve your goal. • Create strategies for implementing your plan to address short and long-term goals. • Accurately assess the progress you are making toward your goals and adjust your actions as needed. • Anticipate situations that lead to counter-productive behavior and impulses (e.g., when faced with a difficult task, my impulse is to stop working on the task and "freeze," rather than seeking strategies to overcome the obstacles to success). • Overcome obstacles to success by identifying resources (e.g., people, information, etc.) that will help you overcome those obstacles (seek help when needed). • Identify those situations that cause personal and interpersonal stress and understand how you react to stress. • Create strategies to manage stress. • Generate alternatives to counter-productive behavior (impulse reactions). • Accept and learn from failures (e.g., view failures as learning experiences and don't be preoccupied with a setback). • Motivate myself.

At a recent conference for superintendents of schools, a superintendent was sharing her concern about the number of attempted suicides and the number of students sharing suicidal thoughts. This district was one of the top three performing districts in the state; the socioeconomic level of the homes was among the highest in the United States.

Self-manage- ment is the ability to suc- cessfully regulate one's emotions, thoughts, and be- haviors in different situations.

She shared the experience of a student who did not get accepted to the Ivy League college of her choice. The student had outstanding grades, was an active partici- pant in school organizations, and seemed to have all the attributes one would hope for in our children. She was accepted at multiple other highly competitive universities. The student was experiencing suicidal thoughts (dangerous impulses). In her mind, she was a failure. All of her academic and personal successes, her acceptance to top universities, and other achievements were of little meaning. Her entire focus and self-image was caught up in the single "failure" of not being accepted at her first choice university.

Students like this are not able to accurately assess their level of suc- cess and failure. They become singularly focused on a failure, rather than moving on to "Plan B."

Social Awareness

Social awareness is the ability to take the perspective of and empa- thize with others, including those from diverse backgrounds and cultures, and those who have differing ideas. It includes the ability to understand social and ethical norms for behavior and recognize family, school, and community resources and supports. Patterns of immigration and the access to so much information have made our communities in- creasingly multi-cultural, multi-religious, and filled with people who have ideas that are different than our own. Each year, social awareness skills become increasingly important for us to succeed in this environment. Table 1.3 lists specific social awareness behaviors in the left column, and the behaviors people demonstrate when they have obtained social- awareness skills on the right.

Children's lives are filled with opportunities to develop their social awareness. They participate in groups, temples/mosques/churches, scouts, work, school, play dates, and other activities. The checklist in

Table 1.3 Social Awareness Connected to Parenting Practices

Social Awareness	Skills Related to the Competencies
• Perspective-taking • Empathy • Appreciating diversity • Respect for others	• Identify verbal (voice intonation, voice volume etc.) and non-verbal (open or closed body position, facial expressions, eye contact, etc.), and social cues to determine how others feel. • Predict others' feelings and reactions to my behaviors and other situations—recognize that same behavior I demonstrate may elicit different reactions from different people. • Show empathy. • Evaluate others' emotional reactions to varied situations. • Respect others (e.g., listen carefully, accurately, and objectively. • Understand others' points of view and perspectives. • Appreciate diversity (e.g., recognize individual and group similarities and differences). • Identify and use resources of family, school, and community when confronted with new or challenging tasks.

Figure 1.2 can be modified to fit any type of group activity. It can be reviewed by the parent/guardian with the child prior to the activity. After the activity, the child can be asked to self-assess his or her skills, thereby increasing self-awareness of his or her relationship management skills and self-management skills.

Parenting Example: *I Want THAT!*

Now that my four children are grown, they tell me stories of what I didn't know. It sometimes makes me wince when they tell stories about their "terrible" childhood. However, one of my sons, Tim, surprised me one day when he told me something good about a lesson that I had taught him.

Figure 1.2 Self-Awareness of My Skills Working on a Team

About My Teamwork Today	Yes!	So-So...	Not Really
I followed directions.			
I encouraged my teammates.			
I played cooperatively with my teammates.			
I participated with my best effort.			
I asked questions when I needed more information.			
I disagreed but didn't argue with the coach, officials, or teammates.			
I brought all the materials and equipment I needed.			
I sought ways to help others give their best effort.			
I find these things easy to do. Explain why:			
I find these things difficult: Explain why:			
I really like these things: Explain why:			
The person I work best with is: Explain why:			
The goal that I'm working on is: Describe the progress you're making on your goal:			

Adapted from *Social-Emotional Learning in the Classroom.* (Ribas, Brady, Hardin 2017). Originally based on an assessment created by Joyce Silberman, fifth-grade teacher, Newman Elementary School, Needham, MA.

I had just bought my two young sons action figures, plastic creatures that were part of a very large set of action figures. On the back of the package, all 20–30 characters were illustrated. Tim said, looking at the characters he didn't have, "I'd really like this one next." Tim remembered that I told him the pictures were put there to make kids feel "empty." "They put them there so you're not satisfied with what you *do* have, and they show you all the things you *don't* have. When they do this, you can never be happy with what you have because there are so many pictures of what you don't have." Tim said that it was a lesson he always remembers—to enjoy what he has and to avoid the empty longing for *more, more, more* that our culture sometimes gives us.

Relationship Management

Relationship management is the ability to establish and maintain healthy and rewarding relationships with diverse individuals and groups. The ability to communicate clearly, listen well, cooperate with others, resist inappropriate social pressure, negotiate conflict constructively, and seek and offer help. Table 1.4 lists specific relationship management behaviors in the left column, and the behaviors people demonstrate when they master relationship management skills on the right.

Parenting Example

Growing up in the '60s, my older brother and I were often in conflict. Those conflicts often turned physical—nothing more serious than a couple of teeth knocked out (mine) over the years. Our mother had a very specific relationship-management strategy she used with us. Whenever we started to get physical in the house, she would say, "Take it outside so you don't break anything." Given that my older brother always won these physical battles, I soon learned how to manage this situation. I would always be the first out the door and start running. Fortunately, I was faster than my brother. Later in this book, we provide a number of alternative conflict-resolution strategies (different than my mother's strategy) that will enable parents to use the inevitable sibling and friend conflicts to simultaneously resolve the conflict and develop the antagonist's skills of resolving their own conflicts in the future. I had a wonderful mother, but I wish she had this book when we were growing up!

There are tools we can use when working with our children that help

Table 1.4 Relationship Management Connected to Parenting Practices

Relationship Management	Skills Related to the Competencies
• Communication • Social engagement • Relationship-building • Teamwork	• Demonstrate the capacity to make friends and work with colleagues. • Cultivate relationships with those who can be resources when help is needed. • Exhibit cooperative work skills, such as working constructively toward group goals. • Evaluate my own skills to communicate with others (including good listening skills), and adjust as needed to develop and improve my communication skills. • Manage and appropriately express emotions and ideas in relationships with those who can be resources when help is needed. • Provide help to those who need it. • Demonstrate leadership skills when necessary, being appropriately assertive and persuasive, yet open to the ideas of others. • Prevent interpersonal conflict and be able to manage and resolve conflicts when they occur (e.g., determine if you are negotiating in conflict situations so that you can reach common understanding—even if you don't agree. You won't always agree on a solution, but understanding why the other person has taken his or her position is important). • Resist inappropriate social pressures and develop strategies for responding to these pressures.

them understand the *behaviors* that contribute to relationship management. One of the most important skills for anyone to learn is good listening skills. The rubric in Figure 1.3 can be used by parents to teach good listening skills and by children to check their own listening skills. As my children entered the work force I often told them, "You will get much more out of your interactions with others if you listen twice as much as you talk." For one of my children this came naturally. He was always a listener and observer. For my other child, it was a skill she needed to develop, since her impulse was to dominate conversations. All of our children bring "to the table" a different level of relationship skills. As parents, it is helpful for us to be good listeners and observers when our children are in social situations so that we can assess their skill levels and provide guidance as needed.

Responsible Decision-Making

The ability to make constructive choices about personal behavior and social interactions that are based on ethical standards, safety concerns, and social norms requires the realistic evaluation of consequences of various actions and consideration for the well-being of oneself and others. Table 1.5 lists specific responsible decision-making competencies in the left column, and the behaviors people demonstrate when they have acquired responsible decision-making skills on the right.

Table 1.5 Responsible Decision-Making and Parenting Practices

Responsible Decision-Making	Skills Related To Each Competency
• Identifying problems • Analyzing situations • Solving problems • Evaluating • Reflecting • Acting ethically	• Identify decisions one makes at home, school, and in the work place. • Reflect on how current choices affect the future. • Identify problems when making decisions and generate alternatives. • Implement problem-solving skills when making decisions, as appropriate. • Become self-reflective and self-evaluative. • Make decisions based on moral, personal, and ethical standards. • Make responsible decisions that affect the individual and community. • Develop strategies used to resist negative peer pressure. • Negotiate fairly, so that "winning" your point doesn't alienate others.

Figure 1.3 Behaviors for Demonstrating Good Listening Skills

CATEGORY	4	3	2	1	Comments
Attentive Listening	I gave full, attentive listening to each speaker with my eyes, ears, and heart.	I showed attentive listening most of the time.	I showed attentive listening some of the time.	I didn't show attentive listening.	
Comments and Opinions	I withheld my comments and opinions while the other person/people talked, but asked appropriate questions after many presentations.	I withheld my comments and opinions while the other person/people talked, but asked appropriate questions after some presentations.	I withheld my comments and opinions while the other person/people talked.	I didn't withhold my comments and opinions while the other person/people talked, and/or didn't ask questions after any presentation.	
Body Language	I responded with appropriate body language, such as eye contact, nodding to indicate understanding, etc.	I responded with appropriate body language most of the time, such as eye contact, nodding to indicate understanding, etc.	I responded with appropriate body language some of the time, such as eye contact, nodding to indicate understanding, etc.	I rarely responded with appropriate body language, such as eye contact, nodding to indicate understanding, etc.	
Curiosity and Respect	I showed curiosity and respect all the time through body language and questions.	I showed curiosity and respect most of the time through body language and questions.	I showed curiosity and respect some of the time, through body language and questions.	I didn't show curiosity and respect through body language and questions.	

Adapted from Rubistar.4teachers.org, rubric ID 1153873 (May 9, 2005). Copyright ALTEC at the University of Kansas (2000–2008) and *Social-Emotional Learning in the Classroom* (April 2017). Norwood: Ribas Associates and Publications, Inc.

Parenting Example: The Punishment Room (Problem-Solving)

I have twin boys who often tussled over anything—a football, a neat baseball hat, riding "shotgun" (in the front passenger seat) in the car, anything or nothing. Whenever they had a dispute, I sent them to our living room (where there was no TV or distractions), where they'd sit on facing sofas to negotiate with one another. I'd tell them that I'd keep the object of their desire and that they couldn't leave the living room until they figured out how they would share or resolve their differences. Most of the time, after a few minutes they'd come out of the room and tell me, "All set, Mom." I'd ask them what they decided and they'd give me their fair-share result. He gets the hat until after we eat dinner, then it's mine.

I never could figure out how they resolved riding shotgun, because they never ever disputed it for the entirety of their childhood. I called one of my now grown-up sons and asked, "Tim, how did you decide on who got the front seat when you were kids? Days of the week? The date?" "No, we got whole days and took turns, but if we didn't go anywhere in the car, the day didn't count."

Their teacher told me they were great negotiators in their third-grade classroom, and I was delighted to hear that these skills had generalized to their relationships with others. The only problem that emerged from my strategy was that whenever we had company and we used the living room, my sons called it "The punishment room." I'm sure my friends and relatives wondered what terrible things I inflicted on my twin sons in there.

Later in the book you will find an assessment form that parents and children can use to rate their own skill level in each of the areas noted in Tables 1.1–1.5.

The Impact of Social-Emotional Skills on School and Life Success

The journal, *Child Development* (July/August 2017, p. 1157), contained a study that looked at 25 research studies about the impact of social-emotional learning programs and interventions used in schools and in community settings. The study examined various changes that occurred between six and 18 months after students participated in a SEL program. The research included more than 97,000 students.

The programs studied were designed to help students and adults acquire and apply knowledge, skills, and attitudes (such as those listed previously) that enhance personal development, social relationships, ethical behavior, and effective and productive work.

The study looked at children and adolescents from kindergarten through high school. It included a variety of races and range of family socioeconomic levels. It included students in the U.S. and outside the U.S., and from rural, suburban, and urban school districts.

1. Special education referrals decreased six percent (Bradshaw et al., 2009).

2. Academic performance increased by 13 percent.

3. The level of positive attitude toward school increased by five percent.

4. The incidence of positive social behaviors in the classroom increased by five percent.

5. High school graduation rates increased (Felner et al., 1993, Hawkins et al., 2009, Bradshaw et al., 2009).

4. College attendance rates increased almost 11 percent and college graduation rates increased by six percent (Hawkins et al., 2009).

5. Student conduct problems in school decreased by almost six percent.

6. Student emotional distress decreased by almost six percent.

7. Substance abuse decreased by almost five percent (Hawkins et al., 2009).

8. Sexually transmitted disease diagnosis decreased by almost 39 percent (Hill et al., 2014).

Stages Children and Adolescents Travel Through to Master Social and Emotional Skills

One "Lesson" Isn't Enough to Learn a New Skill

No matter what skill we are learning, people need frequent exposure and reinforcement before that skill becomes a regular practice. National Football League (NFL) quarterbacks say that to break a bad habit in their throwing motion takes practicing the new motion 1,000 times. Making that new motion automatic, so that you do it without thinking about it, requires using the motion 5,000 times!

Fortunately, we have found that developing children's academic, social, and emotional skills doesn't take nearly that many exposures. However, it does take more than a few exposures to the new skill before it becomes a permanent part of their repertoire. The same is true for us as parents. By reading this book we are learning some new skills to improve our parenting. Initially, it will require that we think carefully about how we address situations with our children each time we use one of these new skills. However, it will eventually become second nature.

Don't get frustrated with yourself if you aren't an expert the first few times you try something from this book.

To help your child develop his or her SEL skills, it is important to understand the process that all people go through before the skill is completely mastered. Whether the skill is riding a bicycle, making a bed, completing a calculus equation, or being a good listener, everyone will follow the **levels of mastery** described below (Ribas, Brady, Tamerat, Deane, Greer, and Billings, 2017).

This is also true for us. If we are now solving sibling conflicts using the model in this book rather than our previous practice, then we, too, will go through these steps before we become completely competent. Don't get frustrated with yourself if you aren't an expert the first few times you try something from this book. To help your child develop his or her SEL skills, it is important understand the process that all people go through before the skill is completely mastered. Whether the skill is riding a bicycle, making a bed, completing a calculus equation, or being a good listener, everyone will follow the levels of mastery described below (Ribas et al., 2017).

Levels of Mastery

The level of mastery for a skill is the degree to which people have acquired the knowledge and skills that they are learning. The path toward mastery is as follows.

Level 1: Introduction Level of Mastery

The first level is introduction level of mastery, or exposure level of mastery. A person is at the introduction level immediately after the knowledge or skill has been presented or demonstrated for the first time. At this level, there is no expectation that the person will be able to demonstrate mastery of the skill on his or her own. No skill can be learned with "one and done."

> *Whether the skill is riding a bicycle, making a bed, completing a calculus equation, or being a good listener, everyone will follow "levels of mastery.*

Level 2: Guided Practice Level of Mastery

The second level is guided practice level of mastery. At this level, a person can demonstrate the knowledge or skill only with prompting from the parent or another person who can teach the skill. As you saw in the tools above, parents/guardians should explain the skills and give their child time to practice before asking the child to self-assess. The first self-assessment should be guided by the parent/guardian. In the case of you (the parent/guardian) learning the skills in this book, we have written the book so that it serves as your "coach." You will be able to go back and reread about the skill every time you need to be guided in your practice.

Level 3: Immediate Level of Mastery

The third level is immediate mastery level of mastery. At this level, the person can demonstrate the knowledge or skill independently, shortly after it has been explained. Even though a person may be able to replicate the skill "then and there," he or she will not be able do it again after a period of time passes. It is important to remember this stage. When we forget about this stage we often get frustrated with our child because it appears our child has mastered the skill, and then a week or a month later he or she isn't using it. It isn't that the skill wasn't learned. It is that the skill hasn't been mastered beyond this level. The good news is that the skill is still in their brain. A review of the skill by us will bring it back to the child much more quickly than the time it took to teach the skill in the first place.

Level 4: Application Level of Mastery

This level is achieved when the person can demonstrate the skill after a period of time has passed since the skill was taught. For example, a child taught to say "please" and "thank you" at home internalizes the practices and uses them without prompting in the future. Or, there might be the adolescent who can now resolve sibling conflicts without our intervention (see Chapter 3 for conflict-resolution skills). However, they may not be able to transfer these skills in an unfamiliar setting. For example, the adolescent demonstrates the skill with a sibling, but doesn't demonstrate the skill when out with friends.

Level 5: Immediate Application Level of Mastery

Immediate application mastery level of mastery occurs when the child or adolescent can use the knowledge and skill in an unfamiliar or new setting shortly after the presentation of the concept. For example, we may have worked with our child on his or her listening skills when talking to a sibling at the dinner table. And, when confronted with the need to listen in an unfamiliar setting (e.g., when in a group of peers), he or she does demonstrate the same skill we taught. However, faced with a similar situation a week or two later in an unfamiliar situation, the skills are no longer evident.

Level 6: Application Level of Mastery

At this final level, the child or adolescent can demonstrate mastery of the skills after a period of time, in an unfamiliar situation. In the example above of the son working in his father's office, the son was able to use the self-awareness learned in the summer two months later, in the college setting (a different setting then the one in which it was taught).

Figure 1.4 shows the typical progression that students follow as they learn new knowledge and skills. It is important to note the following two factors that make helping children and adolescents master these skills more complex and, at times, frustrating.

Figure 1.4 Mastery Levels of Learning

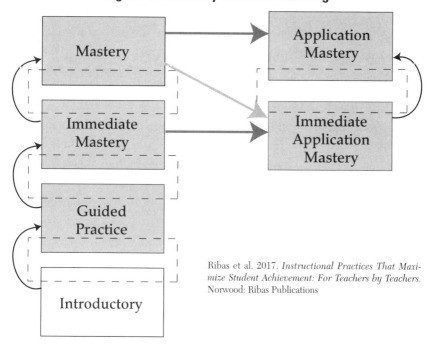

Ribas et al. 2017. *Instructional Practices That Maximize Student Achievement: For Teachers by Teachers.* Norwood: Ribas Publications

1. All children and adolescents *do not* follow the same path to application mastery with every skill. There may be some circumstances in which he or she achieves mastery after the introduction of the skills, whereas for other skills he or she will progress through all the stages in order to master the skill.

2. All children *do not* move through these steps at the same pace (Ribas et al., 2017). Even in the case of twins, who have as close to the same inherited characteristics as you can get and have experienced the same prior parenting practices, there will be a variation in the amount of practice needed to master a skill.

You will note the dotted-line boxes that connect the levels of mastery in Figure 1.4. They represent the fact that the levels of mastery flow into one another, instead of being distinct lines that are crossed between levels. For example, a person moving from guided practice to immediate mastery does so by straddling the two levels, not by taking a step across a line. Upon entering the guided-practice stage, a person may need a very high level of teacher guidance.

As his or her mastery progresses, the level of guidance needed decreases until the person can perform the skill or apply the concept

We should remember that the time it takes to reach each level of mastery will vary depending on the child and the task.

independently (immediate mastery). In some cases, a person can complete the skill independently, but still needs reassurance that the parent or guardian is readily accessible for support. Some people would consider this person at the immediate mastery level, while others would consider him or her still at the upper end of guided practice.

It is important to keep in mind that all people, no matter their age, need to pass through these stages to have a permanent change in their skill level. And, we should remember that the time it takes to reach each level of mastery will vary depending on the child and the task.

Conclusion

As with academic learning, social-emotional learning is mastered at the highest levels when the skills are developed in all areas of a child's or adolescent's life. These areas include:

1. The home
2. The community outside of school
3. The school, and their policies and practices
4. Classroom practices[1]

Helping our children develop social and emotional skills is a much more natural process than helping them with homework and other academic skills. This is because each day provides us with an opportunity to interact with our children in ways that develop their SEL skills. Unlike academic skills practiced at home, social-emotional skill development is a natural part of good parenting. We just parent the way we have always parented, with adjustments that nurture and develop social-emotional learning. The myriad of typical parenting interactions we have each day with our children are all opportunities to develop their SEL skills. As seen above, and as you continue reading this book, you will understand how natural it can be to change our practice to more effective practices.

---

[1] Those parents wishing to learn more about classroom practices that develop social-emotional learning may wish to read the book *Social-Emotional Learning in the Classroom: Practical Guide for Integrating All SEL Skills into Instruction and Classroom Management.*(Norwood, Ribas Associates and Publications, Inc., 2017).

Discussion Questions

1. Think of a job you might like your child to have as an adult. Skim again through the tables with the five skill areas (self-awareness, self-management, social awareness, relationship skills, responsible decision-making). Which do you think is the most important (they are probably all important, but which do you believe is the *most* important) for success in that job?

2. Which of the five SEL skills areas is the strongest for your child? Go back and read the skills of successful people associated with that skill area. Give an example of something your child did that reflected one or more of the skills.

3. Which of the five SEL skills areas is the area where you think your child is in need of the most development? Go back and read the skills of successful people associated with that skill area. Choose one skill of successful people that you think you can help your child develop. What is the first step you can take toward helping him or her develop that skill?

4. Which of the five SEL skills areas would you like to work on to better develop it in *yourself*? Why?

5. Look again at Figure 1.2, "Self-Awareness of My Skills Working on a Team." What is a group or team activity in which your child is involved? How might you use some or all of that figure to help your child improve his or her skills as a teammate?

References

Bradshaw, C. P., Zmuda, J. H., Kellam, S. G., and Ialongo, N. S. "Longitudinal impact of two universal preventive interventions in first grade on educational outcomes in high school." *Journal of Educational Psychology* 101 (November 2009): 926–927. https://doi.org/10.1037/a0016586

Collaborative for Academic and Social-Emotional Learning. "Core SEL Competencies." http://www.casel.org/core-competencies/

Durlak, J., Oberle, E., Taylor, R., and Weissberg, R. "Promoting Positive Youth Development through School-Based Social and Emotional Learning Interventions: A Meta-Analysis of Follow-Up Effects." *Child Development* 88 (July/August 2017): 1156-1157.

Eddy, M., Reid, J. B., Stoolmiller, M., and Fetrow, A. (2003). "Outcomes during Middle School for an Elementary School-Based Preventive Intervention for Conduct Problems: Follow-Up Results from a Randomized Trial." *Behavior Therapy* 34, no. 4 (Autumn 2003): 535–552. https://doi.org/10.1016/S0005-7894(03)80034-5

Felner, R. D., Brand, S., Adan, A. M., Mulhall, P. F., Flowers, N., Sartain, B., and Dubois, D. L. "Restructuring the Ecology of the School as an Approach to Prevention during School Transitions: Longitudinal Follow-Ups and Extensions of the School Transitional Environment Project (STEP)." *Prevention in Human Services* 10, no. 2 (December 1993): 103–136. https://doi.org/10.1300/J293v10n02_07

Hawkins, J. D., Kosterman, R., Catalano, R. F., Hill, K. G., and Abbott, R. D. "Effects of Social Development Intervention in Childhood 15 Years Later." *Archives of Pediatrics and Adolescent Medicine* 162 (December 2008): 1133–1141. https://doi.org/10.1001/archpedi.162.12

Hill, C. J., Bloom, H. S., Black, A. R., and Lipsey, M. W. "Empirical benchmarks for interpreting effect sizes in research. *Child Development Perspectives* 2 (2008): 172– 277. https://doi.org/10.1111/j.1750-8606.2008.00061

Weare, K. and Nind, M. (2011). "Mental health promotion and problem prevention in schools: What does the evidence say?" *Health Promotion International* 26 (Dec 2011) i29–i69. https://doi.org/10.1093/heapro/dar075

Yoder, N. Research-To-Practice Brief: "Teaching the Whole Child: Instructional Practices That Support Social-Emotional Learning in Three Teacher Evaluation Frameworks." American Institutes for Research (January 2014). http://www.gtlcenter.org/sites/default/files/TeachingtheWholeChild.pdf

2

Beliefs about Intelligence and the Acquisition of Academic, Social, and Emotional Skills

Objectives for This Chapter

At the conclusion of this chapter, the reader will be able to:

1. Explain how to help their children (of all ages) confront and overcome challenging tasks.

2. Explain the role of genetics and learned skills as they relate to school, work, and life success.

3. Explain the social and emotional skills (SEL skills) possessed by successful people and how to help their children develop these skills.

Psychologists, educators, and philosophers have studied and debated for centuries the definition of intelligence. Closely tied to the debate on intelligence is its role in people's success in life and their ability to learn new skills. In this chapter, we have provided a short history of the evolution of the beliefs of professionals as to what causes intelligence and its role in life success and skill development. We go on to talk about how the beliefs of parents and guardians can impact the acquisition of SEL skills by the young people they are raising. Chapter 1 explained a complex set of social and emotional skills that provide significant benefit when possessed by an individual. However, skill development is, in part, impacted by the beliefs of the one teaching the skill and the one learning the skill.

In an increasingly diverse society, our children will need to apply these skills to a wide array of people.

To understand beliefs about learning and intelligence, we must begin with ourselves—the first set of beliefs to consider when adjusting our parenting to promote SEL in our children is our own belief system. If we don't have a clear understanding of:

1. Our strengths and weaknesses in these skill areas, and

2. Our beliefs about the ability of people to learn new social and emotional skills,

we will have difficulty helping our children develop their self-awareness, self-management, responsible decision-making skills, relationship skills, and social awareness. Key among these understandings is how our belief system impacts how we interact with our children when helping them develop these and other new skills.

Our Beliefs about "Appropriate/Successful" Behavior Skills

What we believe about the following five areas affects every interaction that we have with our children. We need to have a clear idea of what we believe leads to social, emotional, school, work, and life success if we are to help our children succeed.

1. What constitutes appropriate and/or successful behavior in various social settings?

2. The impact of innate intelligence and learned strategies and their role in acquiring new skills

3. The impact of race, socio-economic background, country of origin, religion, and other factors

4. An increasingly diverse society in which our children will need to apply these skills with a very diverse array of people

5. The most effective way to parent

These beliefs have an impact on the relationships, responses, and expectations that we hold for our children throughout each day.

Our Children's Belief Systems

Another set of beliefs we need to understand and consider are the those of our children. At all ages, children have beliefs that are already established, including their beliefs about their own intelligence and self-worth, and the intelligence and self-worth of their peers (including their ideas on race, socioeconomics, religion, countries of origin, and disabilities). These beliefs have been well established by their prior interactions with us, siblings, friends, acquaintances, the media, their school, and other forces.

More on Our Beliefs

Social-emotional learning must begin with us, parents and guardians, before we can have maximum impact with our children. Each of us operates with a belief system on two levels. The first level harbors our **cognitive beliefs** (conscious beliefs). It's what we learned about positive parenting through our observations and other experiences. These are the beliefs we try to follow. An adult's choice to follow the requirements of a certain religion and/or expect their children to follow those requirements is an example of a conscious belief.

The second level relates to our **unconscious beliefs**. This is how we react to people and situations when we don't have time to clearly reflect on a problem situation, weigh alternatives, and choose the best alternative based on our cognitive belief system. Our unconscious beliefs are the result of how we were parented, educated, and supervised at work; of our religion or culture, or even personal trauma. In the stress of daily life, our unconscious beliefs may control our parenting decisions as much or more than our cognitive beliefs.

For example, one of the authors of this book grew up and attended school in a neighborhood where most families lived in poverty or slightly above.

Many of the parents of my friends (including my father) never finished high school and no one had a college degree. It wasn't until high school that I had friends whose parents had college degrees and white-collar jobs. I was always awed and intimidated by these families. My conscious and unconscious belief was that people who lived in big houses, better neighborhoods, had college degrees, and worked in white-collar jobs were smarter than those of us from lesser circumstances. Over the years—as I acquired college degrees and spent more time among educated, white-collar professionals—my conscious belief system changed. I learned that intelligence and achievement was more the result of hard work than of a family's socioeconomic level. My conscious beliefs changed with time and experience.

My unconscious belief system, however, was much harder to change than my conscious belief system. In 1995, I became an assistant superintendent in a school district that had one of the highest parent education levels and one of the highest family income levels in the United States. Despite my Ph.D. from Boston College and being one of the leaders of an elite public school system, I still struggled with the unconscious beliefs that had been ingrained in me during childhood and adolescence.

I always battled feelings that I was inferior to the doctors, lawyers, CEOs, college presidents, and others with whom I now interacted daily. My unconscious belief was that they had more cognitive, personal, and interpersonal intelligence than me. As I look back at my sixteen years as a classroom teacher, vice principal, principal, and assistant superintendent, I wonder how those unconscious beliefs may have negatively affected the people with whom I worked and my own children.

One of the reasons it is important to understand our unconscious beliefs (increase our own self-awareness) is they can impact our daily interactions with people, often without us knowing it. Our children watch everything we do and learn from our actions as much as they do from our words. Our social-emotional beliefs (both conscious and unconscious) impact our interactions with family members and others in our lives. Our children take lessons from those interactions that they observe.

You shouldn't drive yourself crazy wondering and worrying about what you might be saying and doing unconsciously that may impact your children. You don't need to start psychoanalysis so you can understand your unconscious belief system! Your children are going to learn important positive lessons from the strategies you learn in this book. Also, just the fact that you are reading this book will increase your social-emotional learning and positively impact the behavior you model, both consciously and unconsciously.

There is a physiological reason for regressing to our unconscious beliefs even when they are inconsistent with our conscious beliefs. This typically happens when we are feeling stressed. This phenomenon is probably more prevalent when responding to our child's misbehavior than at any other time in our work as parents/guardians. Our brain is made up of three primary parts: the **brain stem**, the **paleocortex**, and the **neocortex**. In Frederick Jones' book, *Tools for Teaching* (2013, Kindle version), and in Martha Davis's, Matthew McKay's, and Elizabeth Eshelman's, book, *The Relaxation and Stress Reduction Workbook* (2008), the authors discuss the impact on our brain when we are confronted with a stressful situation. For those interested in learning more about these parts of the brain and how their functions impact SEL skills, please read Chapter 5.

How Stress Impacts Our Parenting

Parenting is stressful for parents and guardians, in part because we have so much less control over our children's behavior than we do over our own. As children get older, we have even less control. Added to this is our strong desire for our children to do well in school, work, and life. Confronted with misbehavior or other behaviors we want them to change; ideally we would want to be able to calmly and rationally assess the situation, draw on our acquired knowledge, generate alternatives, assess each alternative, and select the alternative that is best suited to the situation at hand. These are the steps to making a responsible decision.

To do this, we need to operate in the higher level of our brain, the **neocortex**. Unfortunately, when confronted with a stressful situation, the brain's physiological response is to prepare for either **flight, fight, or freeze**. This response has been conditioned in us through millions of years of evolution. The blood leaves the neocortex and the paleocortex and flows to the brain stem and into large muscles.

This unconscious response by our brain prepares us well to flee or fight. Or, it can even cause us to freeze and not respond because the decision-making parts of our brain are impaired by lack of blood. It serves us poorly when we're trying to solve complex problems such as parenting situations. We respond by avoiding (self-awareness), becoming aggressive (relationship skills and social awareness) or resorting to conditioned responses (self-management), rather than using our cognitive belief system and problem-

Parenting is stressful, in part because we have so much less control over our children's behavior than we do over our own. As children get older, we have even less control.

solving skills to deal with the situation (responsible decision-making). As a parent or guardian, the sooner we become self-aware that a parenting situation is inhibiting us from making the best parenting decision, the more likely we are to kick into our "cognitive override" and make a better decision.

It is important to note that this physiological response is also true for our children when they are afraid, angry, or confronted with other stressful situations. Developing their self-awareness of their reaction to stress helps them use "**cognitive override**"[1] so that they can make good personal decisions. It is easy to see why, in times of heightened tension between parent and child, both parties can react with less productive behaviors that can elevate the conflict.

When responding to behavior that we want to help our children change, we need to be cognizant of whether our unconscious parenting responses tend to be **authoritative** or **authoritarian**. Ferlazzo (2015) describes the difference between these two behaviors as follows:

- Being authoritarian means wielding power unilaterally to control someone, demanding obedience without giving any explanation for why one's orders are important.

- Authoritarian responses can lead to the parent/guardian "winning" the immediate situation. However, it does not have any impact on developing the child's SEL skills.

- Being authoritative, on the other hand, means demonstrating control but doing so relationally through listening and explaining.

Opting for the authoritative style will make a child or adolescent more likely to respect your authority and probably more willing to cooperate. **Most parents and guardians believe they should be authoritative rather than authoritarian in our parenting.** Unfortunately, some of us can slip into an authoritarian tone when we are under stress.

> *Opting for the authoritative style will make a child or adolescent more likely to respect your authority and probably more willing to cooperate.*

---

[1]   *Cognitive override* is a phrase we coined. It refers to using self-awareness to avoid making bad decisions based on our unconscious reactions to situations. We stop the impulse and make good cognitive decisions about how to react to the situation.

Intelligence and Skills Development: The Nature-versus-Nurture Debate

Working effectively with our children requires that we closely examine our conscious and unconscious beliefs about intelligence and skill acquisition and how they are acquired. As shared earlier, one author's own conscious beliefs about intelligence, and particularly about intelligence and poverty, took a great deal of education and experience to change over a period of many years. The unconscious beliefs were slower to change. And, since they are unconscious beliefs, we still may maintain some vestiges of earlier beliefs and may not be aware of it. In recent years, we have become more aware of unconscious beliefs contributing to "subtle racism," "myths about poverty," and subtle cultural and religious stereotyping.

These beliefs are not just the result of our experiences in our personal lives. They are the result of hundreds of years of mistaken beliefs. Below we will briefly describe some of that history.

Growth Mindset and Fixed or Deficit Mindset

For more than 130 years, educators, social scientists, and psychologists have debated the question of whether intelligence is innate (an entity) or acquired (**growth mindset**). It is part of the age-old nature-versus-nurture argument that continues to this day. In this next section we look at these two perspectives on the nature of intelligence and how they affect beliefs about cognitive, interpersonal, and intrapersonal intelligence and skill acquisition. Later in this chapter, we will talk more about growth mindset.

An "entity belief" is the belief that *all or most of our intelligence is genetic and a single entity that can't be changed*. Theorists in this school of thought say there is relatively little that we can do to influence the intelligence of a child once they are school age. This is also known as the **fixed mindset**.

A growth mindset is a belief that *intelligence is learnable and multifaceted and can be developed incrementally*. More recently, this theory has revolved around what psychologists call grit and growth mindset. The proponents of this school of thought believe that most of a person's school, career, and life success (up to 75 or 80 percent, say some psychologists and educators) is the result of environment (school, home, and others), effort, acquired strategies for thinking and learning, and the person's attitude toward success and failure. Hence, the term "growth mindset."

Is Intelligence Due to Home and School Environment or Primarily Due to Heredity?

A Short History of How We Arrived at What We Believe Today

As early as 1869, British scientist Francis Galton wrote the book *Hereditary Genius: Its Laws and Consequences*. In it, he spoke about genetics as the primary determinant of intelligence. American psychologists extrapolated from this the concept of **Intelligence Quotient (IQ)**. This was a measurable intelligence that was native and stayed constant throughout a person's life (Devlin, Fienberg, Resnick, and Roeder 2002, p. 2).

In their book, *Intelligence, Genes, and Success* (Devlin et al., 2002, p. 5). the authors describe Galton's work:

Galton was a central figure in the founding of the **eugenics** (a term he coined in 1883) movement. Eugenics was the study of the relationship of heredity to race and talent. From his analysis of biographical dictionaries and encyclopedias, he became convinced that talent in science, the professions, and the arts ran in families so that it would be 'quite practicable to produce a highly-gifted race of men by judicious marriages during several consecutive generations' (Kelves, 1985).

It is interesting to note that Galton was a cousin of Charles Darwin and was influenced by his cousin's work as it appeared in Darwin's famous book, *On the Origin of Species by Means of Natural Selection*. If evolution was the result of the survival of the offspring of the fittest, then isn't it logical that intelligence is something handed down to the offspring of the "smartest"? For the next 150 years Galton's and Darwin's work were among the foundations of the belief by many that intelligence and success were primarily hereditary.

The Role of Intelligence Testing in Promoting the Idea of Hereditary Intelligence

The person best known for developing a measurement for intelligence was Alfred Binet, a psychologist in France between 1894 and 1911. The first intelligence test described by Binet and a colleague in 1896 involved counting objects in pictures, noting similarities among familiar objects, filling in missing words in sentences, and describing how terms had different meanings (Devlin et al., 2002, p. 9). In 1904, Binet was asked to develop a way to determine which French school children needed extra help. He introduced his method for measuring a child's performance against the trends of other children in 1908. His system measured a child's *This was the first step in developing the concept of intelligence quotient or IQ.* mental age in relation to the child's physical age. This was the first step in developing the concept of intelligence quotient or IQ (Perkins, 1995, pp. 23–26).

Binet, despite his work on measuring intelligence, was not a proponent of the idea that intelligence was a fixed, single entity that was established at birth. Perkins (1995, p. 29) describes Binet's reticence to reach this conclusion:

> He [Binet] did not jump from the fact that some people behave more intelligently than others to the presumption that there was one essence, a single mental resource, that some people had more of and some less … He feared it would offer educators (and others) the excuse to ignore the plight of poorly performing students on the grounds that they lacked the intelligence to do better. It also might give people grounds for dismissing under motivation and behavior problems as symptoms of low intelligence.

In *Modern Ideas about Children* (1909, p. 6), Binet stated:

> A few modern philosophers … assert that an individual's intelligence is a fixed quantity, a quantity which cannot be increased. We must protest and react against this brutal pessimism … With practice, training, and, above all, method, we manage to increase our attention, our memory, [and] our judgment, and literally to become more intelligent than we were before.

Binet said this in 1909! It appears from his words above that growth mindset (a.k.a. learnable intelligence) has been around much longer than many of us thought. It has just taken nearly a century to enter into the mainstream of belief about intelligence.

Henry Goddard authored the first American version of an IQ test in 1908 and administered it to 2,000 school children in Vineland, N.J. It was the Americans, between 1908 and 1925, who took Binet's individually administered intelligence tests and turned them into paper-and-pencil, group-administered tests. To do this, they created a single entity IQ score to replace the mental age and chronological age scores developed by Binet, which were difficult to interpret. Stanford University psychologist Lewis Terman imported Binet's test to the United States and developed the Stanford-Binet IQ test (Gould, 1995, quoted by Fraser, 1995, p. 1).

Terman recognized that if IQ tests had to be administered one-on-one by a trained psychologist, they would be too expensive to use widely. He and graduate student William Otis developed the first Army Alpha test that was administered to 1.7 million army recruits between 1917 and 1919. That test would eventually be renamed the Armed Services Vocational Battery and was used during World War II. A version of it continues to be used today by all branches of the military service (Devlin, Fienberg, Resnick, and Roeder, 1997, pp. 9–10).

The data derived from the Alpha tests began to drive the belief in American society that certain cultures were genetically more intelligent than others. Based on the findings from the Alpha tests, Princeton psychology professor Carl C. Brigham wrote the book, *A Study of American Intelligence* (1923). Brigham concluded that the immigration of southern and eastern Europeans to the United States would lower "native" American intelligence. One year later, Congress passed the Immigration Restriction Act of 1924, which enabled a disproportionate level of immigration by northern and western Europeans, who were thought to be more intelligent. In the United States, Supreme Court case Buck v. Bell in 1927, the court supported sterilization laws passed in 16 states between 1907 and 1917. In that opinion, noted Justice Oliver Wendell Holmes wrote, "Three generations of imbeciles are enough" (Hernstein and Murray, 1994, p. 5).

Now, nearly 100 years later, it would be nearly impossible to find anyone who believes that people of Italian, Greek, Spanish, Southern French, or Portuguese ancestry have genetically inferior intelligence.

However, this mistaken belief was endemic, even among the most educated Americans in the first quarter of the 20th century.

In 1912, German psychologist W. Stern improved on Binet's format for determining IQ. Stern (Perkins 1995, pp. 26–28) developed a system in which a person's mental age was compared to his or her biological age. An IQ of 100 meant the person's mental age was the same as the person's biological age. A person with an IQ over 100 had a level of intelligence higher than the average for people with the same chronological age. This

Figure 2.1 The Bell Curve

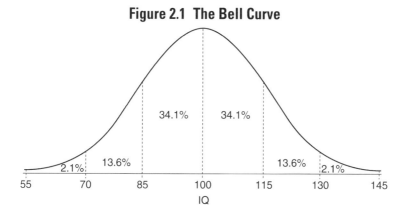

gave rise to the bell curve with which many of us have some familiarity today (see Figure 2.1).

Stern's method worked well for children but became a problem when applied to adults. The mental versus chronological age comparison no longer worked when applied to people in their 40s and 50s. Another method was needed that might be applied to adults and children. Today, psychologists still use a bell-shaped curve such as the one in Figure 2.1. In today's model, IQ is no longer determined by comparing mental age to actual age. Instead, it is normed against the results of many people who are tested to determine average scores and the various levels above and below the average. The number 100 continues to be used for the average score solely to be consistent with Stern's model. A difference of 15 points[2] is used to determine each level of difference.

In the general population, more than 68.2 percent of people have an IQ between 85 and 115, which would be deemed average. Another 13.6 percent of the population have an IQ between 115 and 130 or above average. Another 2.1 percent of the population have an IQ between 130

---

[2] Called a standard deviation by statisticians.

In the 1930s and '40s, the majority of people still believed that intelligence could be defined by a single score, was genetically inherited, and varied by race or culture.

and 145. Only 0.2 percent of the population have an IQ above 145. The same is true for the left side of the distribution, with 13.6 percent of the population having an IQ between 85 and 70, 2.1 percent with an IQ between 70 and 55, and only 0.2 percent with an IQ lower than 55.

In the 1930s and '40s, the majority of people still believed that intelligence could be defined by a single score, was genetically inherited, and varied by race or culture. Most believed IQ was fixed at birth and could not be changed.

Intelligence as Having Multiple Components That May Be Enhanced by Home and School Factors

In 1957, psychologist Ann Anastasi noted at meetings of the American Psychological Association that the nature (entity)-versus-nurture (growth mindset) debate about intelligence had subsided because geneticists, psychologists, and social scientists had become convinced that nature and nurture were interactive and interrelated as they pertained to intelligence. In 1958, she indicated in an article in *Psychological Review* that the focus on the study of intelligence must be on the interaction of both nature and nurture (Anastasi, in Devlin, Fienberg, Resnick, Roeder, 1994, pp. 197–208).

As the 1960s approached, most educators believed that some part of intelligence (or lack thereof) was developmental and not hereditary. Lyndon Johnson's Great Society program brought the program Head Start to schools in high poverty areas to reverse the negative impact of the home environment in socioeconomically deprived homes. The belief was that early intervention would enable students to "catch up" intellectually with their peers from socioeconomically advantaged homes.

Nevertheless, educators and parents were not ready to let go of the concept that intelligence was fixed at some point early in a child's life.

The late '70s through the '80s and '90s brought an increased belief in the malleability of intelligence based on home and school environment. Innumerable examples now exist of highly successful people who, early in their lives, were *not* seen as having a high level of intelligence. We now know that their success was the result of hard work and acquired skills and knowledge.

The genesis of the idea that intelligence is a composite of multiple components came from Alfred Binet. David Perkins credits Binet with presenting us with the first suggestion that there may be multiple intelligences:

> Binet looked at a great variety of kinds of human behavior to gauge intelligence. … He tested children every which way, and the more ways the better. So long as the task did not depend much on unusual rote knowledge or reading and writing it was fine with Binet. … He took this approach because he believed that intelligence, far from being one thing, was a potpourri, a mix of this ability and that ability all jumbled together (p. 25).

For the next 50 years, Binet's thoughts about intelligence containing multiple components were largely ignored as psychologists, educators, and social scientists strove to find ways to establish a person's innate intelligence as a way of socially engineering aspects of society, including the military, education, and the workforce. As stated earlier, the largest body of work in this area at the turn of the 20th century was for efficiently determining job classifications for the military. Schools used the results to determine effective means of tracking students for efficient instruction.

In the 1970s, University of Pennsylvania psychologist Jonathan Barron examined the relationship between strategies and intelligence. Baron's studies looked at the memories of mildly developmentally delayed children versus those of children with average intelligence. In his 1978 article "Intelligence and General Strategies" (pp. 403–450), Barron showed that the significant gap in the achievement on memory tasks that existed between children with average intelligence and children slightly below average might be closed by teaching those with lower intelligence strategies that enhanced their memory.

Lloyd Humphreys, a psychologist at the University of Illinois at Urbana-Champaign, looked at the changes in the IQ test scores between soldiers tested in 1917 and those tested in 1942. Humphreys found a 15-point increase (one full level) in the scores of those tested in 1942. Humphrey credits that increase to the expansion of public education during those years (Perkins 1995, pp. 77–79).

In the 1980s, University of Virginia psychologist Sandra Scarr examined the relationship between genetics and environment in a series

The research on the variability of IQ continues to uncover new evidence of the importance that school and home environment play in increasing (or decreasing) IQ. of studies using identical twins, chosen because of their identical genetic makeup. Scarr identified groups of twins who were separated at birth and raised in different homes. Scarr's work, combined with that of others, established that IQ was 50 to 60 percent attributable to heredity, with the remaining 40 to 50 percent attributable to nurturing factors.

The research on the variability of IQ continues to uncover new evidence of the importance that both school and the home environment play in increasing (or decreasing) IQ. Eric Turkeheimer, a psychologist at the University of Virginia in Charlottesville (Jacobson, 2003, pp. 40-43), found that the correlation (connection) between IQ and heredity is even lower for children from homes with low socioeconomic status than it is for children in socioeconomically advantaged homes. Turkeheimer's research, based on twins studies, indicates that the connection between IQ and heredity for children from homes with low socioeconomic status is one on a scale of one to 10, with 10 being the highest level of connection.[3] This low connection between heredity and IQ would indicate that the environment, of which school and home are an important part, is a significant component of the factors that shape the IQs of children from disadvantaged environments.

Perkins (1995, p. 61) explains to us that a person's IQ is only 50 percent due to genetics. He further explains that the correlation (connection) between IQ and a person's success in school and in the workforce is approximately five (halfway) on a scale of one to 10. If he is correct, that means that a person's genetic intelligence accounts for only 25 percent of his or her success in school and work. The remainder of a person's success is attributable to learned knowledge, strategies, and effort. This appears to show that 75 percent of a person's school and work success may be shaped by parents, teachers, and other nurturing influences.

---

3   To make this easier to understand, we have revised the numbers to use a 10 point scale, with 10 meaning there is a complete correlation (or one-to-one correspondence) between two things. One, on the other hand, would show very little correlation between two things.
In actual research studies, correlations between two factors range on a scale of 1.0 to -1.0. A 1.0 correlation between two factors means there is a perfect match. A -1.0 correlation indicates that each factor has an opposite correlation. For example, the correlation between a person's height and his shoe size is a positive correlation. On the other hand, the correlation between days when the temperature is zero in a region and the number of flowers that bloom on those days in that region is probably about -1.0.

Learnable Intelligence

David Perkins' **theory of learnable intelligence** looks at intelligence as comprising three components. The first is **neural intelligence**. This is the part of our intelligence that is primarily determined by heredity and only changes because of the physical maturation of the brain—i.e., the *nature* portion of our intelligence. In his book, *Outsmarting IQ* (1995, p. 102), Perkins defines neural intelligence as:

> … the contribution of the efficiency and precision of the neurological system to intelligent behavior. This contribution may involve a single unified factor or some mix of several factors. In any case, it is influenced strongly by genetics and physical maturation.

Another way to look at neural intelligence is that it is the part of intelligence that is impacted by the physical structure of a person's brain. It is important to note that the physical structure can be improved by actions taken by an individual; it is not subject solely to heredity. Studies have shown that older people can reduce the reduction in brain function by doing cross word puzzles, reading, and other activities that "exercise" the brain. It is also true that younger people can increase brain capacity by "exercising" their brain with new learning and skill practice. For those who wish to learn more about how the physical brain works, you will want to read Chapter 5.

The second component of intelligence described by Perkins is **experiential intelligence**. He supports this component of the theory by citing the work of Dutch psychologist A. D. de Groot (Perkins, 1995, pp. 80–81) and others. De Groot studied the similarities and differences between the cognitive abilities of amateur chess players and those of professional chess masters. He found that amateurs and professionals explored future moves with the same level of depth. However, the professionals easily beat the amateurs. To understand the reason for this, de Groot showed players a chessboard with a typical game situation and quickly removed the board from their sight and study. The amateurs could only remember the exact location of a fraction of the total number of the pieces on the chess board. The professionals, on the other hand, could remember *all the locations of all the chess pieces*.

When he repeated the experiment with a random placement of the pieces that would not occur in a game situation, however, the amateurs and professionals had the same level of success in remembering the

This contribution is learned, the result of extensive experience thinking and acting in particular situations over long periods of time.

positions of the pieces. De Groot concluded that the professionals, who played much more frequently than the amateurs, had a much more highly developed memory based on the experience of studying chess pieces during game situations. It was their increased level of experience with the various configurations of pieces as they appeared in games that resulted in a greater ability to remember the location of the pieces during the experiment.

Perkins describes experiential intelligence as:

> ... the contribution of context-specific knowledge to intelligent behavior. This contribution (experiential intelligence) is learned, the result of extensive experience thinking and acting in particular situations over long periods of time. While there may be an initial ability to learn efficiently in a domain (for example, musical giftedness), the accumulated knowledge and know-how of thinking in that domain constitutes experiential intelligence (Perkins, p. 14).

Another way to look at this is that practice not only leads to the acquisition of the skill you are learning. It also leads to more efficient acquisition of skills in the same area. In Chapter 1, we discussed the stages of mastery that people go through when learning a new skill. Experiential intelligence can impact the speed at which two people go through the stages of mastery.

The third component of intelligence is **reflective intelligence**. Perkins (1995, p. 339) describes this as

> ... the contribution to intelligent behavior of strategies for various intellectually challenging tasks, attitudes conducive to persistence, systematicity, and imagination in the use of one's mind, habits of self-monitoring, and management. Reflective intelligence is in effect a control system for the resources afforded by neurological and experiential intelligence, bent on deploying them wisely (pp. 102–103).

In Chapter 4, we look at the role of asking children good questions as a method for developing their SEL skills. We discuss what has become known as higher-order thinking questions. These are questions that push us to think in more complex ways, thereby developing the brain's ability to solve more complex problems. Most of these SEL skills require higher-order thinking by our children. Asking the right questions—ones that stimulate higher-order problem-solving and re-flection—is key to developing their SEL skills. Each time we ask our children to use their higher-order thinking we are further developing their reflective intelligence.

In this model of intelligence, teachers, parents, and individuals have little control over the development of neural intelligence; however, teachers, parents, and individuals have a great deal of control over the development of the experiential and reflective intelligences. Later in this chapter, we will look more at the role of teachers and parents in developing the motivation in students to maximize the growth of their experiential and reflective intelligences.

Teachers, parents, and individuals have a great deal of control over the development of the experiential and reflective intelligences.

A Case of Relationships, Growth Mindset, and Grit That Changed a Life

The following case study is a true story. After you read it you will find an analysis of how personal relationships, grit, and a growth mindset significantly influenced the life of one of the brothers. All three of these areas are closely tied to the set of SEL skills we learned about in chapter 1.

Bob and Joe were brothers who were separated in age by four years. They lived in a public housing project with their parents during the 1960s and early 1970s. They attended an elementary school (K-7) in which most of the students either lived in the public housing project or lived in a large mobile home park. Their mother supported the family with her job as a waitress in a nearby diner where she walked to work each day. She never had a driver's license and they did not own a family car. Their father was an unemployed alcoholic who would eventually die of cirrhosis of the liver when the boys were approximately 15 and 11 years of age.

Bob was the brother who appeared to have more potential for success (or more "intelligence," as some would say). After elementary school, he attended the local public high school from which most graduates went on to four-year colleges. He played on the basketball team and was in college preparatory courses.

Joe was a likable young man who made friends easily and was a cooperative student. He went to the regional vocational high school rather than the high school attended by his brother. At that time in public education, the move to high school was a filtering process. Those who were "smart" enough for college went on to the local public high school. Those who were not went to the technical high school to acquire a trade.

Joe enjoyed his time at the technical high school and became a draftsman. He went to work for a local company. His boss noticed right away that Joe was a hard worker, was personable, and had the potential to advance in the company. He encouraged Joe to go to college. Joe thought about this idea for a long time, because he was unsure if he was "college material." After all, didn't his elementary and middle school teachers indicate he was not college material by recommending vocational high school, rather than the local college preparatory high school?

Joe finally decided he would give college a try. Since he was now married and needed the income from his job, he decided he would start going to college at night. Joe eventually received a bachelor's degree in business administration. His degree, hard work, and encouragement from his boss earned him a promotion in the company. His confidence in his ability to succeed in the professional and academic worlds (as engendered by his boss and some of his college instructors) rose significantly.

Afterwards, Joe enrolled in an MBA program at night while he continued at his job. He completed the MBA and achieved further success in the company. During his MBA work, he developed an interest in business law, since this area of study was most relevant to his current employment. He decided to enroll in a part-time law school program. He completed law school and passed the bar exam. Joe went on to become a successful attorney practicing business law.

What about Bob? During high school, Bob worked as a cook in the diner where his mother waited tables. After high school, he continued in that position. During and after high school, Bob also began drinking alcohol to excess. Bob continued to work as a cook in the diner until his untimely death at the age of 47 due to alcohol-related health problems.

As mentioned, the previous story is true. We provide it as context for the following discussion about grit and growth mindset.

Throughout his life, Joe exhibited what has come to be known as grit. Wikipedia describes grit as the following:

Joe exhibited throughout his life what has come to be known as grit.

Noun: courage and resolve; strength of character

"He displayed the true grit of the navy pilot."

synonyms: courage, bravery, pluck, mettle, backbone, spirit, strength of character, strength of will, moral fiber, steel, nerve, fortitude, toughness, hardiness, resolve, resolution, determination, tenacity, perseverance, endurance"

We would add one other characteristic to Wikipedia's definition: the willingness to **delay gratification**. The gratification that most enjoy after a hard day of work is followed by family time and recreation, in the evening and on weekends.

We see in Joe many of these characteristics of grit. It takes significant grit to do the work required to achieve a bachelor's degree, master's degree, and law degree all while working full time. Many hours of sitting in classes and doing homework, at night and on weekends, takes real resolve when his friends were involved in recreational activities. It took grit to push himself into an academic world that was very foreign to the neighborhood and family life he knew as a child.

We can't measure it, but we can't help believing that the interest and support received from his boss, in what we call an "impactful" relationship, was a factor in his success. Joe's grit may have been enough to achieve as he did.

Joe's Social-Emotional Skills

In some ways, Joe may be the poster child for social-emotional learning. His achievements required the self-awareness of both the strengths he possessed and the weaknesses that he needed to overcome. It takes a high level of self-management to juggle a job, academic work, and career development simultaneously. Operating in the white-collar world of business law required the acquisition of relationship skills and social awareness that were not modelled in his home. His success required making the responsible decision innumerable times over many years to use his time in a way that would forward his academic and career success, rather than in recreational activities.

Let's place the three intelligences (neural, experiential, and reflective) in the real-life context of Bob and Joe. Bob and Joe came from the same parents, so it's likely they had similar neural intelligence. One might even argue that, based on Bob's early school success, his neural intelligence may have even been higher than Joe's. At some point during their adolescence and into adulthood, Bob and Joe took very different paths related to their experiential and reflective intelligences. If we track Bob's life after high school, we might argue that Bob experienced no increase in experiential or reflective intelligence.

Joe, on the other hand, acquired increased experiential intelligence as academic and career building blocks. Joe's acquired knowledge and skills at work and in high school led to a sufficient knowledge base to attend college and succeed in college. His acquired learning in college and in his career led to his ability to succeed when attending graduate school. The learning acquired in the MBA program and at work led to his success when attending and completing law school. The building blocks constructed to this point in academia and in his job ultimately led to a successful career as an attorney.

Reflective intelligence also plays an important role in this story. Joe's decision to attend college at night while working required a high level of self-sacrifice, determination, and the delay of the gratification of free-time activities until some future time in his life. It is the responsible decision almost anyone from any background might make, but it is a decision many people choose not to make.

In this example, Joe increased his experiential intelligence and his reflective intelligence.

To understand this idea better, let's look again at brothers Bob and Joe. Let's assume that the decision for Bob to attend the college preparatory high school was based on his having an estimated IQ above average, along with school grades, Iowa tests, and teacher observations. Let's further assume that Joe's estimated IQ and/or school performance was at the average or slightly below and that this prompted the recommendation that he not attend the college preparatory high school.

If Perkins and others are correct, then 50 to 75 percent of what determined Bob's and Joe's ultimate academic and career achievements (or lack thereof) was attributable to family, school, and other nurturing factors (such as the encouragement of Joe's boss for him to attend college). To take this a step further, we may eliminate home as a factor in this example, because both boys grew up in the same home with the same parents. One might then conclude that Bob's and Joe's career achievements are due to nurturing factors outside of the home.

During the 25 years between Joe's entering ninth grade and his becoming a successful attorney, Joe acquired, on his own, or with guidance from others, the mental capacity to achieve at a high level. He developed the following traits associated with grit:

1. Confidence in his ability to succeed at academic tasks

2. The studying, writing, verbal, and problem-solving strategies needed to succeed in undergraduate, graduate, and law school

3. The perseverance to maintain a full-time job and part-time college study for a span of more than 10 years

4. Confidence in his ability to work successfully in a professional environment

5. The verbal, writing, and problem-solving strategies needed to succeed in both the business and legal professions

6. The motivation to succeed in the competitive environment of business law

More on Growth Mindset

Many of these characteristics can be developed in schools and at home by using strategies for developing a growth mindset. People who hear the story about Bob and Joe are often left asking themselves why Joe worked to increase his experiential intelligence, while Bob chose to take no action in that direction.

Stanford University social psychologist Carol Dweck offers interesting reasons that can be applied to Joe's and Bob's behavior. In her book, *Self-Theories* (2000, pp. 3–5), Dweck indicates that some students respond to challenges with an entity belief in their intelligence. This is a belief that intelligence is a fixed entity and, therefore, if a task is difficult for me to do, it must be because I am not smart enough to do it. This also is often referred to as a deficit mindset because a person is convinced that they are permanently unable to do something.

Other people—those who believe that intelligence is what Dweck calls **incremental intelligence**, or intelligence that may be increased with effort and new strategies—see challenges as interesting problems to be tackled step by step. Mistakes are learning opportunities, rather than failures. Dweck labels this the **growth mindset**. In her research, she found that, contrary to popular belief, some students with low confidence in their intelligence still threw themselves wholeheartedly into difficult tasks and stuck with them to fruition. These students had an incremental belief about intelligence. Other students with high confidence did not want their intelligence tested, and their high confidence was quickly shaken when confronted with a difficult task. These students had an entity belief in intelligence.

In another surprising finding, Dweck (2000, p. 53) found that students who had high achievement during their elementary and middle school years were the most, rather than the least, vulnerable to entity thinking when faced with a difficult task. They worried about failure, questioned their ability, and were likely to wilt when they hit obstacles. The other students, those with a history of lower achievement, developed the capacity to stay with a task even when their initial attempts led to failure.

Making Kids Smarter in Schools

David Perkins tells us that our intelligence is 40 percent to 50 percent learned, and that our success in school and life is at least 75 percent due to the strategies we learn, the effort we exert, and the people who guide the development of these two factors. Clinical psychologist Daniel Goleman, Ph.D., the author of numerous books and articles on emotional intelligence, **estimates that IQ only accounts for between 10 percent and 20 percent of a person's success in school and career** (1999). If Goleman is correct, then 80 percent to 90 percent of success in life is in the control of the individual and the people who affect their lives, such as teachers and parents.

How we interact with children has a significant impact on how they react when confronting unfamiliar and challenging situations. What an exciting prospect for parents/guardians and teachers, who are primarily charged with preparing people for successful lives!

Later in this book, we will share some strategies that parents and guardians can use to help children develop a growth mindset. By that, we mean developing students who:

- Willingly exert more effort to complete challenging tasks
- Use strategies to more efficiently learn new knowledge and skills
- Use strategies to solve problems

- Stick with problems until they are solved
- Believe in their abilities to succeed in school and life by applying effort and strategies

Below is a simple technique for assessing whether individual children have an entity or incremental approach to their intelligence. The following questions are based on the work of Carol Dweck and Claudia Mueller (Dweck, 2005, Mueller and Dweck, 1997, pp. 59–62), and our own work with hundreds of children in schools. The questions can be used to do a quick assessment of students' beliefs about the nature of intelligence. The questions are geared toward pre-adolescents, adolescents, and adults; however, it may be simplified or given orally to younger students.

Examining My Attitudes Related to Intelligence

1. Think of a person whom you consider smart. It might be someone you know personally or know from the news or another source. What does this person say or do that causes you to think of him or her as smart?

2. How much of being "smart" has to do with natural ability and how much has to do with learning?

3. Is there a time when you have felt dumb? If so, what were you doing that made you feel this way?

4. Are there times when you feel smart? If so, when?

5. What activities are you "smart" about or good at doing?

6. Choose one of the activities from number 5 above. What percentage of your skill in this area is due to the intelligence/ability you were born with? What percentage is due to your working hard and gaining the skills?

Those who believe we have a fixed intelligence tend to answer the questions by attributing success or failure mostly to innate intelligence. Those who believe intelligence can grow, tend to attribute success to effort and acquiring skills. This has become known as **attribution theory** (Heider, 1958).

By retraining people to think of intelligence as something we acquire with hard work and strate-gies, we develop in them the desire to work on challenging tasks to completion.

Attribution retraining is the process of getting a person to the belief that hard work and acquired skills are the primary reasons for success. By retraining people to think of intelligence as something we acquire with hard work and strategies (growth mindset), we develop in them the desire to work on challenging tasks to completion. We motivate children not to give up when something is difficult, but to learn from their mistakes and try again (see Figures 2.2 and 2.3 below).

Implicit or Unconscious Bias and Confirmation Bias

Up to this point, we have discussed beliefs as they relate to intelligence in general. Some of the more troubling beliefs can be confounded by conscious or unconscious beliefs about race, socioeconomics, religions, or gender.

Tests of implicit bias (or unconscious bias) show that people of all backgrounds show unconscious preferences on the basis of gender, race, sexual orientation, or other aspects of identity. According to these tests, most people favor the group they are a member of—despite claims that they have no preference. The tests also show, however, that people across groups show preferences for the "culturally valued group." Approximately one-third to one-half of the people in "stigmatized groups" tend to favor the "culturally valued group" (Morin, 2015, pp. 4–7).

You will remember we talked about the attitudes many American scholars held toward southern Europeans at the turn of the century. Most believed that southern Europeans had genetically inferior intelligence. Of course, nearly all of those scholars were northern Europeans!

This type of gender and cultural bias exists today. One author describes his experience with this dynamic as follows:

I spent my first two years of teaching in a high-poverty school. I taught second grade one year and third grade the following year. After me, the first male teacher any of the students saw was in fifth grade. Each year the principal would assign me all the boys "who needed a man" —a.k.a. the boys who couldn't behave. I thoroughly enjoyed and had success with these boys the others found highly frustrating or uncontrollable. This was for two reasons. The first is that as an elementary student I consistently received "D" (low) grades in conduct because I couldn't sit still or keep my mouth shut. I was a "frequent flyer" in the principal's office. The second is that my female colleagues had all been "good girls" in school. They couldn't understand why these boys behaved as they did. They assumed the behavior of these boys was a choice they made to disrespect the teacher.

It is difficult to teach self-management, self-awareness, social awareness, and relationship skills if you don't understand the underlying reasons why these skills don't exist. In schools, boys represent 79 percent of preschool children suspended once, and 82 percent of preschool children suspended multiple times—although boys represent 54 percent of preschool enrollment. The female teachers with whom I worked were dedicated professionals, but they had a strong unconscious bias regarding the behavior of boys. We now know more about the differences between boys and girls that contribute to boys being less able to "behave" than girls.

Below we discuss some differences between boys' and girls' brains during brain development.

A Look Inside Girls' Minds

Gurian and Stevens (2004, 2010) found several characteristics of girls' minds that affect student learning. These are:

1. The **corpus callosum**[4] of a girl's brain tends to be larger than that of a boy's, thus allowing more "cross-talk" between the two different hemispheres in the girl's brain.

2. Girls tend to have stronger neural connectors in their temporal lobes than boys do. Thus, **these connectors allow girls to have more sensory detailed memory, better listening skills, and the ability to more easily distinguish between different voice tones.** In addition, this difference between boys and girls allows girls to use greater detail in writing assignments.

---

[4]   Those interested in learning more about the brain and its role in social-emotional learning will want to read Chapter 5.

3. Girls tend to have a larger **hippocampus** (a memory storage area in the brain) than boys, which gives girls a learning advantage, particularly in the language arts.

4. Girls' **prefrontal cortex** is more active than that of boys and it develops at an earlier age, thus allowing girls to have better impulse control than boys. In addition, girls tend to have more serotonin in their bloodstreams, which also makes them less impulsive.

5. Girls tend to use more cortical areas of their brains for verbal and emotive functions, whereas boys tend to use more cortical areas of their brains for spatial and mechanical functions.

Although these are just some of the characteristics that define a girl's mind, understanding these factors helps us better understand why girls generally do better than boys in reading and writing in their early school years (Conlin, 2003, in Gurian and Stevens, 2004, 2010). In contrast, because the girl's brain devotes more of the cortical area to verbal and emotional functioning, it does not use as many of its cortical areas for abstract and physical-spatial functions as does a boy's brain. This difference may, in part, explain why fewer girls are interested in physics, industrial engineering, and architecture early on. Children are drawn to activities that their brains find pleasurable. By *pleasurable*, we mean "in neural (brain) terms, the richest personal stimulation. Girls and boys, within each neural web, tend to experience the richest personal stimulation differently" (Gurian and Stevens, p. 22)."

It is important, however, to note that this does not physiologically limit the ability of people to obtain high skill levels in all areas. Early language acquisition by girls does not mean boys can't catch up.

It is important, however, to note that this does not physiologically limit the ability of people to obtain high skill levels in all areas. Early language acquisition by girls does not mean boys can't catch up. Effort and skills acquisition are much larger factors in a person's ability to succeed in a specific field than these brain differences. These differences will not preclude a girl from being a mathematician or a boy from being a successful novelist.

A Look Inside Boys' Minds

Gurian and Stevens (2004, 2010) have also uncovered several characteristics with regards to boys' brains:

- Boys generally use half as much brain space for verbal-emotional functions as girls do because more of their cortical areas are dedicated to spatial-mechanical functioning. For this reason, many boys gravitate toward moving objects such as balls, model airplanes, or their bodies.

- Boys have less serotonin and oxytocin (the primary human bonding chemical in the brain) than girls do, which makes boys more physically impulsive. In addition, it is more difficult for boys to sit and listen empathetically to a friend (Moir and Jessel, 1989, Taylor, 2002, in Gurian and Stevens, 2010).

- Boys' brains operate with less blood flow than those of girls and tend to compartmentalize learning. Thus, girls are better at multitasking, have longer attention spans, and can transition between lessons and classes more easily (Havers, 1995, in Gurian and Stevens, 2010).

- Boy's brains renew and recharge themselves by entering a rest state, whereas girls' brains can reorient neural focus without ever entering this rest state. Therefore, teachers more often find boys fidgeting or tapping pencils to stay awake. Boys, more so than girls, tend to nod off before completing their work or in the middle of a lecture. Boys generally stay more engaged in a lesson if the teacher uses fewer words and more diagrams, pictures, and movement.

Boys generally stay more engaged in a lesson if the teacher uses fewer words and more diagrams, pictures, and movement.

The qualities that characterize a male's brain explain why more boys than girls prefer to play combat-centric video games and sports. It also explains why boys tend to get in trouble more than girls in school for impulsivity, fidgeting, and boredom, as well as for their "inability to listen, fulfill assignments, and learn in the verbal-emotive world of the contemporary classroom (Gurian and Stevens 2004, p. 23)." This does not mean that girls cannot achieve at equal levels to boys in mathematics and physics. Since effort and skills acquisition are the primary determinant of success, effective effort is more of a determinant of success than gender differences in the brain. The brain differences speak more to the need of approaching parenting in ways that allow both boys and girls to learn, rather than believing that one is "smarter" or "better behaved" than the other in specific areas of their lives.

Growth Mindset, Attribution Retraining, and Student Beliefs about Interpersonal Relationships and Skills

A great deal has been written about growth mindset and attribution retraining as it relates to academic success. They are equally important as they relate to intrapersonal and intrapersonal success at home, work, and in the larger community. As seen in Figure 2.2, children who feel "stupid" will go to great lengths not to look that way to their peers.

There are two common "masking" behaviors. The first masking behavior is to misbehave. It is far more acceptable in the mind of a child or adolescent to be seen as bad by their peers than it is to be seen as stupid. The second masking behavior is to appear uninterested and/or lazy or to avoid the activity completely. Once again it is far preferable in the minds of children and adolescents to be seen as lazy and uninterested than it is to be seen as stupid.

Changing a child's cycle is a process that can be slow in developing. The older the child, the longer it often takes to make the change.

Changing a child's cycle is a process that can be slow in developing. The older the child, the longer it often takes to make the change. **We should remember that the older the child, the longer he or she has operated within a negative cycle that has contributed to the current lack of motivation.**

In Figure 2.2 (starting from top box, clockwise), we see that failure, or the fear of failure, leads to masking behaviors (avoidance, low motivation, and/or disruptive behavior). These masking behaviors then lead to reactions from adults and peers that reinforce the child's belief that he or she is not intelligent (**deficit mindset**), which in turn leads to more avoidance behavior, and so on.

The next part of this chapter looks at the ways we can reverse this negative cycle and create a new cycle, like the one in Figure 2.3. In this

Figure 2.2 Cycle of Low Motivation and the Impact of Deficit Perspective on the Learning Behaviors of Children and Adolescents

Lack of effort because of the belief that my failures are due to an innate lack of intelligence and so effort will not contribute to the same level of success others enjoy.

This reinforces my belief that intelligence is innate and that I was not one of the people with the good fortune to have been born intelligent.

Cycle of Low Internal Motivation

Disruptive and/or avoidance behaviors (e.g., not doing homework) that hide my perceived lack of intelligence behind a message to my teachers and my peers that my lack of success is due to my indifference about learning and my belief that school success is not important (or even to be reviled).

Teachers (and at times parents and peers) respond to my constant display of these behaviors with frustration that leads to a diminished relationship and sends me the message that they see me as "bad" or not intelligent.

Adapted from Ribas, Brady, Tamerat, Dean, Greer, and Billings. *Instructional Practices That Maximize Student Achievement for Teachers by Teachers,* 2017.

cycle, the **impactful adult** (parent, guardian, boss, mentor) implements strategies that start the change. We must remember that the change in the child's behavior will come slowly because there have been a number of previous years in which the old cycle has been nurtured, resulting in deep roots. In some cases, we initially may not see any, or see only small, changes. However, the new cycle we set in motion will move on with the student and benefit him or her in future years.

As parents/guardians, there are specific ways in which we can change this cycle in the classroom. Before we can seriously embark on changing the cycle, we need to raise our own self-awareness of our beliefs related to performance and behavior.

Figure 2.3 Creating a Growth Mindset
and Reversing the Cycle of Deficit Mindset

Lack of effort because of the student's belief that failures are due to an innate lack of intelligence and that effort will not contribute to the same level of success others enjoy.

Teacher has more to praise, continues relationship-building, continues teaching effective effort strategies, continues to use teaching that engages the student and is matched to his/her learning style, and continues community-building.

Teacher uses relationship-building strategies that cause the student to feel liked and respected by the teacher. The teacher uses engaging and differentiated teaching that enables the student to have small successes. The teacher uses effective praise, strategies that teach the student that success is due to effective effort, and uses strategies that build class community.

Reversing the Cycle of Low Internal Motivation

Student expends more effort, acquires more strategies, and has more success.

Student begins to believe he/she can succeed with effective effort, and experiences the good feelings related to success. This results in a reduced need to use disruptive and/or avoidance behaviors to hide his/her lack of perceived intelligence behind a message to the teachers and peers that his/her lack of success is due to indifference about learning and the belief that school success is not important.

Ribas et al., *Instructional Practices That Maximize Student Achievement for Teachers by Teachers*, 2017.

Conclusion

At the heart of what determines a person's behaviors related to self-awareness, self-management, responsible decision-making, relationship skills, and social awareness is their belief system. This includes both their conscious and unconscious belief systems. Becoming self-aware of these beliefs is a prerequisite to changing a person's social-emotional behaviors. As parents and guardians, we can only positively affect the beliefs of children if we have an understanding of our own beliefs.

Developing in our children a growth mindset (as opposed to a deficit mindset) toward the acquisition of their social, emotional, and other life skills will empower them to improve these skills throughout their lives.

It is also helpful for us to understand how children acquire skills. The different aspects of learning, neural, reflective, and experiential aspects give us three different ways to approach developing our children's skills. Understanding the stages that people go through when mastering new skills helps us make learning permanent.

Discussion Questions

1. Define the difference between conscious beliefs and unconscious beliefs. If possible, give an example.

2. Define cognitive override. Give an example of some impulse reaction you have had in your life or your child's life in which the impulsive behavior was not productive. How could cognitive override help to change the impulsive behavior to a more productive behavior?

3. Share a time in your life (or your child's life) when you mastered a difficult task. Share the role that hard work, persistence, and acquiring skills played in mastering that task.

4. Share someone who is an impactful adult in your life (it could be a parent). In what way did this person positively impact your life?

5. Choose one of the skills of successful people (from Chapter 1) that you would like to help your child to improve. Who is the impactful adult best able the assist him/her with developing this new skill (it could be you or someone else).

References

Barron, J. "Intelligence and General Strategies," *Strategies in Information Processing*. ed. Underwood, G. London: Academic Press, 403–450.

Binet, A. *Modern Ideas about Children*. Translator Heisler, S. Menlo Park, CA: Suzanne Heisler, 1975 (original work published 1909).

Davis, M., McKay, M., and Eshelman, E. *The Relaxation and Stress Reduction Workbook*. Oakland, CA: New Harbinger Publications, 2008.

Devlin, B., Fienberg, S., Resnick, D., and Roeder, K. "Heredity, Environment, and the Question of How?" *Psychological Review* 65 (1994): 197–208.

Devlin, B., Fienberg, S., Resnick, D., and Roeder, K. "Intelligence and success: is it all in the genes." *Race and Intelligence: Separating Science from Myth* (2002): 355–368.

Dweck, C. *Mindset: The New Psychology of Success*. New York: Random House, 2006.

Dweck, C., and Elliot, A., eds. *Handbook of Competence and Motivation*. New York: Guilford Press, 2005.

Goleman, D., *Emotional Intelligence*. Washington, DC: PBS Video, 1999.

Jacobson, M. "Afraid of Looking Dumb," *Educational Leadership* 41 (September 2013): 40–43.

Jones, F. *Tools for Teaching*. Santa Cruz, CA: Fredrick H. Jones & Associates, 2013.

Kelves, D.J. *In the Name of Eugenics: Genetics and the Uses of Human Heredity*. New York: Alfred A. Knopf, 1985.

Ferlazzo, L. "Study: 'Authoritative,' not 'Authoritarian,' Classroom Management Works Best for Boys." Larry Ferlazzo's Websites of the Day…, June 10, 2015, http://larryferlazzo.edublogs.org/2015/06/10/study-authoritative-not-authoritarian-classroom-management-works-best-for-boys/

Gurian, M., and Stevens, K. "With Boys and Girls in Mind." *Educational Leadership* 61 (3) (November 2004): 21–26.

Gurian, M. and Stevens, K. *Boys and Girls Learn Differently! A Guide for Teachers and Parents*, revised 10th anniversary ed. San Francisco, CA: Jossey-Bass, 2010.

Heider, F. *The Psychology of Interpersonal Relations*. New York: John Wiley and Sons, 1958.

Hernstein, R. and Murray, C. *The Bell Curve: Intelligence and Class Structure in American Life*. New York: The Free Press, 1994.

Morin, R. "Exploring racial bias among biracial and single-race adults: The IAT." Washington, DC: Pew Research Center, 2015.

Perkins, D. *Outsmarting IQ: The Emerging Science of Learnable Intelligence*. New York: Free Press, 1995.

Terman, L. "Were We Born That Way?" 44 *World's Work* (1922): 657–659.

U.S. Department of Education Office of Civil Rights Civil Rights Data Collection: Data Snapshot. http://ocrdata.ed.gov/

3

Resolving Conflicts and Other Important Conversations with Your Child

Objectives for This Chapter

At the conclusion of this chapter, the reader will be able to:

1. Plan ahead for important discussions with your child to insure you achieve the goals of your conversation.

2. Use "effective praise" to maximize your child's acquisition of social-emotional (SEL) skills.

3. Use "descriptive feedback" to maximize your child's acquisition of SEL skills.

4. Explain the difference between punishments and consequences, and use consequences effectively.

5. Guide important conversations with your child through stages to maximize your child's acquisition of SEL skills.

6. Facilitate the resolution of conflicts between your child and friends or siblings in ways that model skills the child can use to resolve future conflicts.

Planning for Important Conversations with Your Child

For most parents and guardians, the ability to talk with your child seems like an easy task. However, as children age, events and problems may occur that create the need for a deeper-level conversation. Some of these discussions may have something to do with a discipline or behavioral issue, with difficult peer interactions, or with an event that impacts the family. The goal of building good communications skills with your child or adolescent is to strengthen the SEL skills identified in Chapter 1: **Self-awareness, self-management, social awareness, responsible decision-making,** and **relationship skills.**

Below are questions we may want to ask ourselves prior to discussions with your child/adolescent:

1. What do I want to be the end result of the discussion? What do I want my child to know and/or be able to do when the discussion ends? For example, are there certain behavior changes I want as an outcome of our talk? Are there skills I hope my child can take away from this discussion? Every conversation with our children is an opportunity to help them develop social-emotional (SEL) skills. Many of us assume that we can begin a talk with our child about important topics and develop the direction of the discussion while talking. In many cases, this does result in a positive outcome. However, at other times, it is best to plan ahead to insure it goes well. Even those who are skilled at impromptu discussions may find their effectiveness increased by planning ahead.

2. How will you know if the discussion succeeded? Is there a way you can determine what impact it had at the conclusion? For example, did you summarize the key points of the discussion? Did you ask your child to summarize what he/she takes away from it? How can you determine if the discussion had a *permanent* impact on his/her behavior? Is there a way for you to monitor behavioral changes over time? Many answers may not be easily or immediately discerned; it may take days, weeks, or longer for children to process and internalize lessons or ideas from the talk.

3. How will I initiate the discussion to maximize my child's willingness to listen and participate? Where and when is the most opportune time to initiate a conversation like this? For example, will I wait until my child or adolescent is home by himself or herself? Should I initiate a conversation when the child/adolescent seems upset about an incident or should I wait until he/she calms down? Is there a special phrase or sign that I can use to determine my child or adolescent's willingness to talk to me?

4. How do we want the discussion to progress to maximize my child's understanding of what was discussed? Is there a way to tell if I am "getting through to my child?"

5. How will I end the discussion to achieve these objectives:
   a. Insure common understanding of what was discussed
   b. Increase the likelihood of the long-term success of what was discussed
   c. Protect and nurture my relationship with my child as he or she goes forward?

The most important idea is to create opportunities for frequent dialog with your child. If you can create opportunities for conversation while your child is young, then it may assist you in establishing a pattern of communication between parent/guardian and child as he/she matures. Parents/guardians must be aware that it is never too late to attempt to improve your ability to communicate with your child as you help them develop his or her SEL skills.

In the next section, we will look at the way we construct the language we use in these conversations. Much has been written—based on research and practice—about the best "phrasing" to get optimal results when talking with children and adolescents. In the next section we will look closely at the language categories of **praise**, **recommendations**, and **descriptive feedback**.

The Importance of Praise (the right kind!)

Focus on "Praising the Process," Not Just the Completion of the Task!

The first language category is **praise**. One goal of giving praise is to make the child feel good about his or her performances that were successful. There are two larger types of praise.

One sub-category is what we refer to as **general praise**. This includes statements such as "good job," "excellent," "awesome," etc. Although this kind of praise is pleasant to hear, it is one-dimensional and does little to encourage a child to strive for improvement. General praise is not instructional; i.e., there is nowhere else for you to go to get better. General praise doesn't provide any specific information about how the child got to where he or she is. It is by better understanding the above process that people are able modify and improve their behavior.

The second sub-category is **specific praise**. This kind of praise includes a description of what is praiseworthy. "I noticed that you let your brother have the last cookie; that was really kind." "Thank you for clearing the table without being asked; I appreciate it." This type of praise provides a much clearer idea of where they are and where they are going. This approach increases the chance of more positive behavior change then general praise. An example of specific praise may go something like this: "That was a tough game today, but I noticed that you really moved the ball down the field." Or, "That drawing looks really good. Your eye for detail is really impressive."

Use specific praise more often, as it turns unconscious competence into conscious competence.

It is recommended to use specific praise more often than general praise as it turns **unconscious competence** into **conscious competence**. Unconscious competence refers to when we do something well but don't understand or recognize the specifics of what we did that made it effective. For example, some adolescents are better observers and listeners than others. One parent described his two children who had very different levels of competence with learning by listening and observing the behaviors of others. One child is a very good listener and observer with his peers and at work, using the information to improve his situation. The other likes to dominate conversations with her peers and colleagues. She talks much more than she listens when with a group.

The good listener always had competence in listening and observing, but never realized he was doing it or its value. On several occasions, when this was witnessed by one of his parents, they would point out his skills in this area and the value the skills brought to him. He had unconscious competence that was raised to conscious competence. By making the unconscious conscious, he is better able to replicate the skill in the future.

One can imagine this when complimenting a child or adolescent in this manner. "Jamal, you really have a great voice. I was noticing it the other day when you were singing in your room." Jamal may appear to be a self-conscious about this comment; however, he may then become more conscious of this skill, as a result he might try out for the chorus in school or church.

When children compliment friends at school, they might say, "Hey, man, you can really draw!" The child or adolescent often takes more pleasure in this kind of statement because he/she was recognized by a peer. When we help a child or teen move toward conscious competence, we are helping him or her become more self-aware and improving his/her understanding of social awareness in the family and the wider world.

There are additional sub-categories of praise. There is **congratulatory praise**; another is **encouragement praise**. Congratulatory praise tells the child, "You have arrived" in a particular area of performance competency. An example might be praising a child for obtaining a good grade on a test or for winning a game. Encouragement praise tells the child that he/she is making good progress toward the final task or goal but is not yet where he/she needs to be.

We can use the analogy of learning to ride a bike—how training wheels serve as a physical manifestation of encouragement praise. As children attempt to learn and then master new skills, parents find that encouragement praise is very beneficial in helping children grow in confidence.

Helping children learn how to cook and prepare simple meals are great ways to practice these skills. Parents or guardians can start by encouraging children to help wash the lettuce, or (with supervision) to heat something in the microwave. Once the child masters some early skills, parents and/or guardians might find a cookbook for kids and employ different kinds of praise to inspire the child to prepare part of a family meal. I remember making tuna burgers from a cookbook created for kids and being very proud of my accomplishment. Think how encouraging this kind of behavior could help the entire family!

What are some examples of encouragement praise? Imagine that you are teaching your child to build something, perhaps a tree house or a race car for a scouting derby. The first attempt with a hammer might be awkward, but it is helpful to encourage the child with comments like, "That's good, Mike. Hold the hammer like this. Now, give the nail a tap. Do you think the board will hold on the tree? Let's see how it looks!" After the parent/guardian and child have an opportunity to examine their work, the parent/guardian may think that there needs to be some correction to the work. Here is how encouragement praise might sound under these circumstances:

Parent: "I think it looks pretty good, Mike, but I am worried that some of those boards may not hold. What do you think we could do to make it more secure?" This approach demonstrates respect for the child's opinion and also helps the child brainstorm some ideas on how to improve the construction of the project. Once the child states some of his or her ideas on what to do, the parent/guardian might respond by saying, "That sounds like a good idea. Let's try it out and see if it works." This type of approach may also strengthen another of the SEL skills identified in Chapter 1. The child is working toward a goal, in this case building a tree house. The child or adolescent may also increase his/her ability for perspective-taking as he/she works along with a parent/guardian on such a project. Both parent and child trying to learn and respect one another's view.

The task of teaching a teen to drive can tap into many SEL skills, including self-awareness. The task of teaching a teen to drive can tap into many SEL skills, including **self-awareness** (accurately recognizing one's strengths and limitations). Adolescents often have an inflated sense of their driving ability and can be antagonistic when being corrected. Parents and guardians are most helpful if they remain calm and offer encouragement praise, such as: "You are doing really well for a new driver." "Keep some distance between his car and yours." "Good job; you are really making great progress." An added benefit of offering to be the driving coach is additional one-on-one time with your teen. This can be a great opportunity to share thoughts and feelings about all kinds of things that might be important to your child, and it can help improve communication between parent and teen.

It is essential to identify the adult who is best suited for the task. It may be a parent, grandparent, guardian, or a mature older sibling who has the best temperament for this task. A nervous or tense passenger can cause more anxiety to the fledgling driver, and this will not create a positive outcome for either parent/guardian or novice driver. Teenage drivers need a lot of practice with a calm and encouraging adult to help them grow in competence and confidence.

When trying to support and encourage a teenager who is learning to drive, it is essential to show some enthusiasm. It might go like this: "So, Greg, I know you have to get some driving hours this week. Let's try to go on Sunday afternoon for a couple of hours. How does that sound?" The majority of teenagers will jump at the opportunity to get in some of their required driving hours. Another benefit—the parent/guardian can offer *calm* guidance. "Okay, Greg, put on your blinker and let's ease onto the ramp. That was a nice, smooth turn."

Self-management is the ability to seek help when needed. Your adolescent will need to ask for help as he/she attempts to fulfill his or her driving hours and negotiate the use of a car. Asking for help can be difficult for some teens because of the need to demonstrate their independence from a parent/guardian. Learning how to drive creates an easy opportunity for the teen to ask for assistance. In addition to self-awareness and self-management, teaching a teen to drive also offers opportunities to discuss and improve upon another SEL skill: **responsible decision-making**.

Parents or guardians and professional driving instructors must reinforce the importance of driving safely. Currently, one of the most pressing concerns is reminding teens not to text when driving. This is a conversation that must be repeated often—but parents/guardians must also be aware of their own behavior around this. If the parent often talks on the phone or texts while driving, the child receives mixed messages.

Some responsible decision-making skills are: identifying the decisions that one makes at school and in the rest of life, reflecting on how current choices affect the future, and discussing strategies to resist peer pressure. These skills are essential as children grow into adolescence and move away from parental/guardian scrutiny. Unfortunately, there are too many stories in the news that illustrate the tragic events that can happen when someone—adolescent or adult—fails to make responsible decisions. When driving with a child, the parent/guardian can refer to these stories to initiate a discussion of the dangers of texting or drinking. However, many adolescents have a sense of invulnerability that makes this challenging.

The attitude of "it won't happen to me" is hard to overcome but engaging in this conversation frequently is essential. The conversation might go like this: "Athena, I need to talk to you about the rules of the road: there can be no texting and no drinking while driving and do not drive with a friend who texts or drinks when they are driving. Let's figure out a way that you can always reach me if you need a ride or if you are worried about being in a bad situation."

This is an opportunity for the parent/guardian to establish a safety pact of sorts. The adolescent and parent/guardian agree on a code or strategy that allows the teen to save face with peers, while also letting the parent/ guardian know the child needs help. This signal or code could alert the parent/guardian that the teen needs to be picked up from a party or a potentially dangerous situation. In general, it is advisable to save intensive questioning of the adolescent until the next day and to focus on getting the child removed from the situation. It is also advisable to discuss strategies that the teen can utilize should the parent/guardian be unavailable for a pickup. For example, who else could they call? Establishing a protocol is comparable to establishing a family escape plan in the event of a fire. If the teen is aware of what he/she can do in an emergency, he/she is more likely to implement the plan.

Importance of Sports and Other Activities

Involvement in a team sport or a club can reinforce the SEL skill **relationship management**. For example, team sports, dancing lessons, scouts or being a member of a club or church, temple or mosque youth group can help children and adolescents exhibit cooperative learning and work toward group goals. These experiences help children learn cooperative skills and loyalty. These types of extracurricular activities also assist with developing responsible decision-making and a code of ethics that goes beyond simply scoring more points than your opponent on the field or beating an adversary on a chess team. Group activities can benefit both physical and emotional health, and children can shine in areas that are outside the academic demands of school. Involvement in a variety of experiences helps children become more well-rounded and grow in self-confidence. The overall benefit can be an improved quality of life and social well-being.

Involvement in a team sport or a club can reinforce relationship management.

Although all children appreciate praise, depending on the age of the child the nature of the praise will vary. As children age, the parent/guardian must be careful about over-praising a child in front of siblings. Children are often quite competitive with their siblings, so parents/guardians must be conscious of providing positive comments and praise to *all* members of the family. Accordingly, they must endeavor to find opportunities to recognize each child.

Parents and guardians must also avoid labeling their children. Here are some examples of labeling: "Oh, that's Mary. She always gets the good grades. She's our brainiac." Or, "Jackie, oh, she's our middle child. She is not the best student, but she is so pretty." Or, "Jake, he's the jock of the family. He doesn't care too much for reading, but he sure can play any sport!" When parents /guardians praise or recognize a child for a single attribute, it can limit the child's growth and relegate him or her to a particular role they then play in the family dynamics. Children are seldom one-dimensional, so finding ways to recognize all their talents is essential in helping them see themselves as individuals with multiple capabilities and possibilities. For example, Mary may be a great student but she is also involved with the nature and loves to garden. Jackie may get a lot of attention for her appearance, and this can be a source of stress and conflict for a young girl. But when parents or guardians make note of her ability to write poetry or her love of animals, or her kindness to others, this will help Jackie view herself as a full person with interests, hobbies, and other wonderful attributes that have nothing to do with her appearance. Jake is a great athlete, but he is also a very responsible young man who works at a part time job where he is viewed favorably by his boss and his customers. When parents/guardians recognize the different dimensions of their children, they are contributing to helping their child with the SEL skill of self-awareness.

Finding ways to recognize all their talents is essential to helping children see themselves as individuals with multiple capabilities and possibilities.

Some children appreciate the public acclaim of recognition; other children, especially adolescents, may be uncomfortable or even embarrassed by the attention. At younger ages, they do not possess the self-awareness to know how they react to praise. It is a good opportunity to help them gain self-awareness about situations that trigger different emotions.

Once children reach adolescence, parents and guardians must be very aware of praising them in front of their peers. And, teenagers may be very embarrassed by public displays of affection or too much praise in front of friends. With some children, a note in a lunch box that offers "Great job" or "Thinking of you—good luck on your test!" may be the best way to let a child know you are there for him or her. Often, just being present at their sporting events, recitals, school performances, or shooting hoops at the neighborhood court, are physical examples of **encouraging praise**. Due to their work schedules, some parents/guardians have limited opportunities to partake in these events, so finding a time at the end of the day to check in with your child is very helpful. It might sound like this: "Taisha, I just wanted to see how your day went. I know you had that project due today. How did it go? Tell me something you found interesting that you learned from doing the project."

The Importance of Expressing Gratitude

Helping a child learn the importance of gratitude is an example of developing the social-awareness SEL skill. A related skill is identifying verbal and physical social cues in order to determine how others feel. Parents/guardians can model expressing gratitude by acknowledging when a child does something without being asked.

For example, a parent or guardian might say, "Thanks for walking the dog when you got home. That was really helpful because I didn't get a chance to do it earlier." Or, "Thanks for starting dinner without being asked. We will all be able to eat together tonight because of your effort." Expressing gratitude is a powerful habit to impart to a child and makes the child feel that he/she is contributing to the family.

When the parents/guardians demonstrate gratitude in their daily interactions within the family, children tend to emulate that behavior. It is equally important to offer an apology to your child or adolescent if the circumstances require it. Perhaps you had promised to attend a game or another event, or said you would take your child to a movie or to shoot hoops. We all know that unexpected things may happen—at work or because of a family emergency—that can force us to break a promise. A sincere apology to the child or teenager can go a long way in building trust between parent/guardian and child. "Tyrone, I know we were supposed to get pizza together today, but I have to attend a meeting at work unexpectedly. I am really sorry about this because I know you were looking forward to it. Can we reschedule?"

As long as a parent/guardian does not disappoint the child or adolescent too often, the relationship will survive these occasional disappointments. However, if canceling plans with your child/adolescent happens too frequently, the child will feel that he/she cannot trust the adult and their relationship will suffer. When parents and guardians practice their own social-awareness skills with their children, they show how empathy and respect are essential, positive attributes of communication.

Recommendations

The second language category is **recommendations**. Recommendations should tell a child both what needs to be improved and how to improve it. Recommendations come in two sub-categories: **suggestion recommendations** and **direction recommendations**.

Suggestions are recommendations that are optional for the child to implement. For example, you might *suggest* that your child tackle his or her homework as soon as he/she gets home from school. However, the child may prefer to wait until after dinner or some other time. As long as the work gets done and the child isn't staying up beyond his/her bedtime, there may be no need to move to a *direction* recommendation. Another instance of when a suggestion recommendation might be called for is when your son or daughter is deciding what to wear for the school picture. The child may be in love with his/her "Super Hero" costume or a band T-shirt. The parent/guardian might suggest that the child's school picture will last a long time but his/her attachment to the Super Hero or band may change.

A *suggestion* recommendation may also refer to how parents/guardians encourage the completion of household responsibilities, e.g., washing the dishes, taking out the trash, or cleaning his/her room. However, if children do not follow through on their responsibilities, then the parent/guardian might need to move to a *direction* recommendation. A direction recommendation is more specific, creates more detailed guidelines with regard to a task, and is not "optional." For example: "I know you are having school pictures tomorrow. The school sent home some information that they want you to follow with regard to your attire. Do you need or want some help selecting what you will wear?"

The above approach will be more accepted by younger children than with middle- or high-schoolers. With older children, the direction recommendation might go like this. "I know you are having your picture taken for school tomorrow. The school sent home a list of guidelines about what is appropriate and what is not going to be acceptable for school portraits. Have you decided what you will wear? Let's see if your choice coincides with what the school is saying. If your first choice turns out not to be appropriate by the guidelines, what might be your other choice?"

Notice how the parent/guardian does not directly dictate that attire, but uses the information provided by the school as a guide. In addition, the parent/guardian uses language that is respectful of the child and includes him or her in the decision process. "So, if your first choice isn't going to meet the guidelines, what is your second choice?"

This approach can also assist the child in developing another SEL skill, responsible decision-making. Parents/guardians should also keep in mind that adolescents really like a sense of self-reliance. When possible, allow your child to have some options of what we refer to as **controlled choice** before you move on to a more direct recommendation. For example, "Sean, I know you have that project due in a week. Do you want to go to the library today or tomorrow?" Creating choice opportunities often increases the rate of compliance. The key is to make sure that you (as parent and or guardian) are comfortable with either choice.

Providing Descriptive Feedback

The third language category is **descriptive feedback**. In everyday language, the word *feedback* typically refers to anything we tell a child about his or her performance. *Descriptive feedback* refers to a more specific type of feedback language used by parents. It is nonjudgmental, observable evidence about behavior and its impact, and it helps the child assess his/her own behavior. Descriptive feedback comprises neither praise nor recommendations, nor does it contain any judgment from the parent or guardian. It can be the most powerful technique for instigating positive change in a child's behavior. Its effectiveness is that the child can assess his/her own performance against a "target performance," and then judge how he/she can improve.

If the target performance is for young Mary to keep her papers in a specific place, ready for the next school day, the descriptive feedback might sound like this: "Mary, when you came home from school today, I noticed that you left your homework all over the kitchen counter. What do you think you might do to get ready for tomorrow morning?"

This is a low-conflict situation but it is an example of nonjudgmental feedback that provides children with the opportunity to examine their own behavior and to figure out how to correct it.

Descriptive feedback can be the most powerful technique for instigating positive change in a child's behavior.

Here's another example that might be familiar with older children. "Jose, you were the last one who used the car last night. Today, when I wanted to go to work, the gas tank was almost empty, causing me to have to stop and get gas and making me late for work. I am not feeling inclined to let you take the car again. What do you think you could do that would change my mind?" This is a mid-level conflict situation, but again, it provides an example of nonjudgmental feedback and enables the adolescent to think about consequences and decide on possible solutions that will avoid negative consequences.

This approach will help fortify his responsible decision-making because he reflects on how certain choices affect his future, e.g., "If I don't fill up the car once I am done using it, I may not get to use it later."

Parents and guardians should also keep in mind that adolescents really like to feel a sense of self-reliance. When possible, allow your child to have some options in what we refer to as **controlled choice** before you move on to a more direct recommendation. For example, "Sean, I know you have that project due in a week. Do you want to go to the library *today or tomorrow*?" Creating controlled choices often increases the rate of compliance. The key is to make sure that you (as parent and or guardian) are comfortable with either choice.

Descriptive Feedback in Conversations with Children

Here is an example of a high-level conflict that might arise with an older child or adolescent. This scenario is challenging because the potential for emotional reaction is higher on both sides: "Mike, you broke curfew last night. I called you and texted you and didn't hear anything back from you. I need you to understand how this caused me to be very worried. I thought something really bad might have happened to you."

Mike may respond in various ways. *Denial:* "I wasn't that late; you guys worry too much." *Excuses:* "My battery died." Or, "I had to drive someone home unexpectedly." *Pushback:* "You guys are always on my back! I'm 17. What's the big deal?"

At this moment, it would be easy to escalate this exchange into an argument. Sometimes, the best strategy is to "table" a confrontation until the next day. Before the teenager makes plans to go out with his or her friends, arrange to have a brief discussion about the expectations of curfew and remind the child that adhering to a specific time will be directly related to his/her freedom to meet up with his/her friends. This may be a topic that will resurface, because that is the nature of adolescents, but being prepared for these kind of conversations does help.

High-level conflicts require more patience and strategic intervention than low-level ones.

Each of these situations requires a different kind of response. The high-level conflict situations require more patience and strategic intervention than the low-level conflict situations, but getting comfortable with how to discuss and work through the low-level situations, helps to build a more positive communication pattern with your child, thus helping both parent and child work through the social-emotional challenges of adolescence. When parents/guardians employ descriptive feed-back, it helps children better understand what they discover through their own analysis. They will feel more ownership for the recommendations. This increased ownership increases their motivation for implementing the changes identified through the observational process.

Sometimes we have to move from everyday casual conversations to important discussions with a child or adolescent. There may be an incident at school or outside of school that predicates this need and so we will need to prepare and thoughtfully carry out the discussion. Below are a series of steps that can help to succeed in these circumstances.

Difficult Discussions with Your Child

Step 1. What to Consider in Advance

Imagine that the school calls to tell you that your child was involved in a bullying incident. Your first reaction might be embarrassment or anger. Having a conversation immediately with your child might go something like this: "Jimmy, I can't believe you were involved in a bullying incident! How could you do this? Haven't we taught you that bullying is wrong?"

This approach will shut down any communication with your child because, although it is a very understandable reaction, you have not allowed the child to provide his/her explanation first. Now imagine this approach: "Jimmy, I need to talk to you about something very important. The school called me today and told me that you were involved in a bullying incident. I was very upset to learn about this! I would like you to tell me what happened."

At this point, the parent or guardian must employ great patience and active listening. The child may be embarrassed or angry. The child may have been bullied previously by the bullying victim. You must try to obtain all the information about the incident before you decide on the best response. Make sure that you confer with someone at the school whom you feel would be able to provide an unbiased description of what happened that caused this event. For example, a teacher or lunch room monitor may have observed part or all of the altercation—but not the precipitating event.

It is difficult to hear anything negative about one's child but it is important to get all the information before determining the appropriate consequence. What if the situation involves a disgruntled neighbor complaining about some vandalism or a call from the police? Parents and guardians must try to remain calm and get as much information as possible from these outside sources.

Many years ago, I held a party in my home and while the party was taking place, my son and a few of his buddies thought they would paintball one of the cars parked outside on the street. My friend called me the next day to alert me that someone had paint-balled her car while it was in front of my house. I had an idea what might have happened, and asked my son and his friends if they were responsible for what happened. After some squirming and avoiding my eyes, they admitted that they had been responsible. I drove them to that person's home and they apologized for their behavior and meticulously washed and vacuumed her car. The offended party graciously accepted their apology and, to the best of my knowledge, this group of kids did not partake in that particular activity again!

The Value of Family Meetings

Family meetings are a useful tradition to establish as a method of increasing communication and harmony in the home. A family meeting can provide an efficient and positive way to develop SEL skills among all participants. If a parent or guardian has never tried this kind of approach before, then it may take a bit of convincing about the need for such an event. Ideally, you may want to "sell" the idea to your children by keeping the initial attempts less confrontational, e.g., "We want to plan a family vacation and want to hear what you want to do." They can address a change in family dynamics: "Grandma is going to move in with us and we want to talk about how you feel about this."

If a parent/guardian gets into the habit of having regular family meetings, then the children and adolescents are used to this tradition and are more comfortable sharing their thoughts and feelings with both their parents and their siblings.

What is the best way to establish a family meeting? Ideally, you will first discuss with your family that you want to arrange a special time and place to talk as a group.

If the children are older, then have everyone bring their schedules to arrange several times during the week when everyone could meet for at least 30–60 minutes. Some families have weekly meetings and it is woven into the fabric of family life. In past years, many families ate dinner together every night, which offered an opportunity for regular conversation. Today, many families run on such different schedules that they might challenge an air-traffic controller. Thus, arranging a set day and time for a family discussion is preferable.

If this is something that you have not attempted before, it is advisable to have an agenda about what will be discussed at the meeting, making sure that you include time for all members to have time to share their thoughts and concerns. Sometimes, you may be able to resolve a family problem in one family meeting, but often you may have to consider it as the first step toward a satisfying outcome.

If something that will impact the family's structure is about to happen, e.g., a divorce or a serious illness, then, for the well-being of all family members, it is important to continue to discuss how these circumstances will affect life in the household.

For example, if the father has just received a diagnosis of terminal cancer, this will drastically affect the family. It will change the emotional and financial stability of the family. The children might have had some idea about seriousness of their father's illness, but including them in details about his treatment and ways in which they can be helpful is beneficial. After the initial shock and dismay of the news, the children may feel soothed by learning how they can take on chores that had previously been done by their father.

Due to the serious nature of this kind of situation, family meetings need to be held over the course of the illness, as the needs in the family continue to change. The family meeting also created a safe space for the children and adolescents to share their feelings of sadness and anger over the events that had transpired.

In general, children and adolescents do better if they are informed about a situation rather than being kept in the dark about issues that directly affect them. When children are not included in these important discussions, it may increase their levels of fear and anxiety about what is going on. However, parents/guardians must also be prepared for possible reluctance, or even refusal, to participate in this kind of meeting. Aim first for *physical* presence, then work on *verbal* contributions. As children become accustomed to this approach, they are more likely to improve their involvement over time.

Step 2: Choose the Location

Depending to the age of your child and the importance of the discussion, choosing the right location for a discussion is key to gaining the most beneficial outcome. William Pollock, author of *Real Boys: Rescuing Our Sons from the Myths of Boyhood*, says that "Girls are sensitive to shame, but boys fear it" (1998, p. 129). Parents and guardians must keep this in mind when arranging a discussion with their child. Pollock also observed that girls tended to be more forthcoming in sharing details about their school day (especially at the younger age) but boys were more likely to say, "Everything is fine."

Pollock says that boys may wait to tell you that something is bothering them, but eventually give a signal that they want to talk. He refers to this as the "timed silence syndrome" (1998, p. 66). For example, a boy might come home from school and go up to his room and shut his door, but poke his head out after a while and ask, "Hey, mom, when's dinner?" This may be a signal that he is more willing to share what is on his mind. He also found that boys were more likely to share their feelings if they were engaged in a one on one kind of activity with the parent or guardian. One mom started shooting hoops with her son and found that during this activity, the son was more forthcoming about what he was feeling.

Parents/guardians can look for opportunities that might be favorable for conversation. In the next section, "door openers," you will read more about locations that are effective for conversations.

Step 3: Use Door Openers

Door openers are a practice that encourages adults, children, and adolescents to participate in a give-and-take discussion. Door openers encourage children to talk and share their thoughts early in the conversation. It helps them feel more comfortable sharing their ideas and feelings. Some conversations are planned for and scheduled, while others are not. Creating a positive atmosphere of good communication, in which children feel their input is valued, must start when children are quite young. Whatever the age of the child, there are always steps that a parent or guardian can take to improve communication with his or her child or adolescent.

In blended families, step-parents must frequently find ways to reach a new stepchild. These delicate relationships can be strengthened or decimated by the tone and comments made by either party. The step-child may rebel when taking direction from a step-parent. The biological parent can get caught in the middle, and everyone ends up feeling upset or disrespected. This is when having a good grasp of the SEL skills in this book can serve as a "GPS" for some of the turbulent issues that can appear.

Some important discussions with children and adolescents take place unexpectedly, due to an event or discipline concern. Parent/guardians must learn to listen and look for teachable moments and opportunities that come up in our daily lives. For example, children see the news and sometimes, intentionally or not, are exposed to horrific events that affect people in far off nations and in their own neighborhoods. I was in a first-grade classroom the other day while students were talking about what they might do if they had super powers. One child said that he would send things to Syria to help the people who were suffering. Older children may be exposed to a lock-down at their school, or view a school shooting, and become extremely upset about this terrible, too frequent,experience. These types of images or lived experiences can be especially difficult for children to understand without the assistance of a parent or guardian to help them process their feelings.

Despite our best efforts to shield children from these events, they are often all too aware of bad things that happen around them. It is important to gauge the emotional "temperature" of your child about such events, because if we avoid talking about these things altogether, children will create their own narrative or become fearful about the world around them.

Some door openers include the following questions:

- What does your child tell you about school?

- What does he or she like best?

- When does he or she feel successful?

- Are there times in school when he or she does not feel successful?

- Whom does he or she identify as his friends?

- What do you think are your child's academic strengths?

- What types of hobbies or activities does your child enjoy outside of school?

What are some other opportunities for door openers? Road trips, even short ones to the store, often create the perfect opportunity for children and adolescents to share their thoughts and feelings. Ideally, this is done with one child and one parent or guardian in the car. Both parties are facing forward and phones should be silenced. This is often when a child will be most candid about what is going on in her/his life. Perhaps you could open the conversation with something like this: "Ned, I noticed that you have not been hanging out with your friends lately and you seem kind of down about that." At this point, you have planted the seed but you must then be quiet and listen. It may take awhile but this opening line can "grease the wheels" that enable a child to start revealing what is truly on their mind. Asking your son or daughter to take a walk with you to the store, or just to walk the dog, can also open opportunities for more intimate conversations.

Carpools and Learning the Scoop

We often serve as chauffeurs for children and their friends during the years of sports team practices, school dances, religious instruction, and the many other activities that take place throughout the school age years. By keeping mum and listening well, you may be able to decipher the social strata that take place during these years. When the driver employs *passive listening* and makes no comments, children often forget that the driver can hear them and will talk candidly about school, other kids, events, etc. Later, you might bring up something you heard in a private moment with your child. "So, Karen, I heard some of the kids mention that Susie's parents are away this weekend and that she is having a party...."

Karen may not want to talk about the details of what was overheard, but a parent/guardian might use this opportunity to discuss why an unsupervised party can lead to all kinds of problems. Perhaps the parents/guardians had a similar experience when they were in high school and could share how a situation that looked like it might be fun initially turned into a problem of property destruction and dealing with the police. This conversation could serve as a chance for the teenager and parent/guardian to develop strategies to use for resisting negative peer pressure—one of the skills for competency in responsible decision-making.

Step 4: Passive Listening and the Importance of Staying Aware

As we mentioned above, parents must be alert to opportunities for **passive listening**. During this step, it is very important to refrain from talking and to give your full attention to your child. For many of us, "listening" is only not talking but also anxiously awaiting our next turn to talk. *We then are more focused on what we want to say next then on understanding what the child is saying* and his or her perspective by putting ourselves "in his/her shoes."

Be aware of your body language and eye contact. If your child feels that you are fully engaged in the process, then he/she is more likely to think you are open to the topic of discussion. Selecting a space where you can sit facing your child may enhance the experience. Then nodding, your comments such as, "I hear you," and "I understand," and your paraphrasing or rephrasing what your child said are beneficial. This approach sends the message that not only are you listening to your child or adolescent, but you are truly *hearing* what they are saying.

You must resist the temptation to interrupt when your child says something with which you disagree. Listening does not necessarily mean that you agree with all the points your child or adolescent is trying to make. It does, however, signal that you respect the process. A passive listening conversation might go like this: "So, Jamal, what I hear you say is that you feel really angry that your sister was able to go to a friend's house but you were not. Is that correct?" The child may continue on with his/her reasons. Then, the parent/guardian may sum up the reasons again: "So, from what you are saying, you feel that it was unfair that we allowed her to go to her friend's house but did not allow you to do that." Again, the parent/guardian waits for the child to respond so as to make sure that he/she has accurately captured the child's feelings. This back and forth—rephrasing and asking for clarification—between child and parent/guardian is the process of passive listening.

In the age of texting, parents must be aware of what kinds of texts their children send and receive. Despite cries from children that accuse parents and caregivers of invasion of privacy, many experts are challenging parents to be actively aware of the negative impact of online bullying and how it can lead to disastrous outcomes. They must be aware that children who seemed fine outwardly but were receiving terrible messages on their cell phones, experienced terrible emotional damage, sometimes leading to suicide. If you are not comfortable looking at your child's phone without permission, you can observe your child's facial expressions and body language as he/she reads and responds to texts. Sometimes this will give you an indication that there is a problem.

Parents and guardians must recognize the influence of technology in their children's lives. In order to protect children from dangerous situations it is essential to help them understand the dangers of "sexting" and engaging in online conversations with people they do not know.

Step 5: Active Listening

Unlike passive listening, which emphasizes the parent or guardian's focused, quiet attention to the conversation, **active listening** gives the speaker tangible evidence of the listener's understanding of what the speaker is trying to convey. Active listening lets them know you are understanding their emotional state and perspective as well as just the words.

One way to do this is to label the child or adolescent's feelings about the situation (e.g., anger, excitement, pride, frustration, confusion).

An active listening session may sound like this: "So, Angela, it sounds like you're *very frustrated* by this situation. You're trying to talk to your teacher about retaking a test and he doesn't want to let you to do it. What were your reasons for asking the teacher for this?" At this point, Angela may offer up her reasons for making this kind of request. The parent/guardian may continue, "Do you think you might approach the teacher in a different way about your request? Why do you think the teacher denied your petition?" Angela may come up with some reasons why her teacher declined her request. "So, if the teacher still does not accept your request for a re-test, what do you think you could do next time?"

Allow a child to think through possible solutions. If the parent/guardian believes that the child does have a legitimate reason for being allowed to retake a test, the parent/guardian can offer to speak to the teacher on the child's behalf. However, it is advisable for parents/guardians to first help the child think through ways in which he/she can learn to advocate for himself or herself.

Wait Time

Wait time, or waiting while your child has time to respond to a question, can be part of the active listening process. Even though he/she doesn't answer right away, it doesn't mean that the child isn't thinking about what you said. Many people's unconscious reaction to silence in a conversation is to jump in and talk—a response conditioned by society. When the conversation stops, it feels uncomfortable; we have the urge to fill the quiet with words. Teachers and therapists understand this, and are taught to use wait time: they wait a few seconds or more after asking a question. They find that when wait time is used, the responses of children and adolescents are longer and more thoughtful.

When wait time is used, the responses of children and adolescents are longer and more thoughtful.

When you first do this, it is likely that both you and your child will be uncomfortable with the silence. It is fine to say "I am giving you some thinking time" so the child knows why you aren't breaking the silence. This form of listening also might be employed when a child wants to make a case for a request. Parents and guardians then encourage the child or adolescent to outline the reasons for their request.

With younger children, this might involve a situation similar to one of the following:

- Being allowed to stay at home alone after school instead of going to an after-school program
- Being allowed to walk home after school by himself or herself
- Being allowed to travel on public transportation with his or her friends
- Negotiating a later bedtime
- Requesting a pet
- Asking to go to a new friend's home or apartment
- Asking to go to a sleep-over party
- Dropping a sport or piano lessons
- Asking for an allowance or an increase in an allowance

With an older child, you might experience this type of situation:
- Getting a cell phone
- Finding and getting a part-time job
- Getting a tattoo
- Dying or cutting their hair in an unusual way
- Getting a new pair of the latest sneakers
- Going on a school trip
- Negotiating a later curfew and being allowed to "hang out" with friends
- Negotiating permission to attend a concert
- Asking for the family car or buying a car of his or her own
- Applying for college (this is frequently a source of great conflict)

Step 6: Generating Solutions for Areas in Need of Improvement

Generating solutions, instead of giving recommendations, is a powerful approach to helping children and adolescents feel they have a voice in solving a problem. People are also more motivated to implement the solution if they feel they were part of its development. The parent or guardian can ask the child or adolescent what ideas he/she has for addressing the identified issue. The child or adolescent can present his/her ideas and the parent/guardian can add his or her own solutions.

An example of generating solutions might be: "Jim, you seem to be having a hard time getting up for school in the morning. I have some ideas that you might use to avoid this, but I'd like to hear your ideas about what you think might help you avoid oversleeping." This is the time to wait and listen before you (parent or guardian) step in with your ideas. Pause, allow the child to think this through and speak. Then you might say something like, "Those are some great ideas. I still have a couple of thoughts that might also work. Would you like to hear them?"

Another example, which might require helpful recommendations from a parent/guardian: Your child is aware of a robbery in the neighborhood and might know the people who were involved. This is a very challenging topic to broach because, out of misguided loyalty or fear for personal safety, the child might feel that he/she cannot "narc on" (tell on) someone. It is a situation where you might need some outside help from law enforcement, a trusted member of the clergy, or another leader from the community. The child must feel that they can reveal this information while maintaining privacy. The parent/guardian might also want to discourage the child from associating with kids who might be involved in illegal activities.

A conversation may go like this: "Grant, I am really concerned about some of the things that have been going on in the neighborhood. What are some things you could do to stay safe?" After listening to your child, you might encourage him/her, "Yes, going to the after school program is a good idea. I can meet you after work and we can go home together."

Discussing Relationships and Appropriate Behavior

Perhaps you have noticed that your daughter (or son) seems to be seeing an older teenager or adult, and you are concerned about the age discrepancy and worry about the kind of pressure this might be putting on your child. Parents and guardians often find that banning such a relationship will cause it to go "underground," which can put your child at more risk.

One strategy for dealing with this is to invite the "questionable friend" to dinner in order to get to know this person. Including this individual can allow you to gain insight into their thinking, and can provide an opportunity for you to express your expectations about how you want your son or daughter to be treated.

It is also important to have an open discussion with your daughter/son about appropriate touching and personal boundaries. This can be a difficult topic—awkward and embarrassing. Parents/guardians can start with age-appropriate comments, such as "Private parts are what your bathing suit covers." In addition, they must be aware that children might be uncomfortable about being told to "Go give Uncle Bill a kiss," or "Give a hug to Mrs. Smith," a visiting neighbor. Situations like these can make both parent/guardian and child/adolescent feel uncertain about the social expectation. The parent may be thinking, "Oh, what is the big deal?" Uncle Bill or Mrs. Smith is very nice and my child should show some affection, etc. However, parents/guardians must pay attention to the comfort level of their child. If the child seems reluctant or uncomfortable by a stranger's attention—even a relative or a neighbor can be considered a stranger to a child—then the parent/guardian can encourage courtesy by shaking hands, rather than insisting on a hug or a kiss.

Many years ago, I was at coffee shop with my then very young children. An older couple came into the restaurant and the man kept touching my son's hair and saying what a cute little boy he was, etc. I will never forget the helpless look on my son's face. He wanted the man to stop, but he also had been raised to be polite to everyone, especially to his elders. While I was self-conscious about confronting this man, I did ask him to stop touching my son. The man became defensive. I then said, "My son is not comfortable with you touching his hair, so please stop." The man's wife urged him to move away. I believe he meant no harm to my child but I learned that my job as mother included protecting my child and showing how to set boundaries about his own person. When parents/guardians demonstrate respect for a child's personal boundaries, this helps the child have a greater understanding of the idea that "Your body is yours, and no one should touch it without your permission." This message helps children develop the essential SEL skill of self-awareness: labeling and recognizing your own and others' emotions, identifying what triggers your own emotions, and identifying your own needs and values.

When parents/guardians demonstrate respect for a child's personal boundaries, this helps the child understand that "Your body is yours, and no one should touch it without your permission."

Children and adolescents should be aware of what is meant by sexual harassment and how it impacts both females and males. Talking very clearly about personal boundaries and appropriate forms of touching have to start early on in a child's life so she/he feels a sense of control over his/her own body. It is crucial to talk candidly with older children and adolescents about posting pictures of themselves online and the long-term ramifications of doing this. Although these kinds of conversations are often uncomfortable for both parent/guardian and child/adolescent, they are essential for children's present and future safety.

A parent/guardian can ask a child or adolescent what he/she thinks about the meaning of sexual harassment. Have they seen examples of this happening at their school or at their job?" This is the kind of topic that will likely need to be discussed over a period of time, and its nature might change as the child grows up.

Step 7: Expanding the Agenda

Sometimes, despite the questions and problem-solving suggestions posed by parents or guardians, children and adolescents may require **concrete recommendations**. For some children, this will be more difficult than it is for others. Especially in the cases of children who have challenges (e.g., nonverbal learning disability or autism spectrum), this step can be essential, as they often miss subtle suggestions. Parents and guardians might need to revisit some of the earlier steps as the child grows towards more autonomy. Even those children and adolescents without a disability may be resistant to solutions because of their denial that a problem exists. This again might require a return to earlier steps in the process.

Here is an example: "Karen, remember how we talked about when you should start your homework? It seems like this is still a problem. I want you to start your homework as soon as you get home from soccer practice. You can have a snack, but plan on sitting down to do homework by 5:30. That should give you a full hour before dinner. Can you repeat the plan for me?" This directive is very clear. However, the parent might also leave a reminder on the fridge that says, "Hope practice went well. Remember, you start homework at 5:30, and I'll see you when I get home from work. There's a snack for you in the fridge." Notice that this is very clear, not punitive in tone, but expands the agenda.

Step 8: Closing the Gap in Perception of Performance

Sometimes, despite our best efforts to communicate with our children by using a joint problem-solving model, we fail to reach agreement or a solution that all of us can live with. There may be a reality gap between our idea of completing an activity and the child's perception of properly completing the it. A simple example of this might be the directive, "Clean your room before you go out." Although, this sounds like a pretty clear request, there can be a gap between what the parent sees as a clean and orderly room and how the child or teenager perceives the same assignment.

Teachers face the same challenge when they tell students to "clean out your desk" or "clean out your locker," or "organize your backpack." Some children and adolescents are naturally orderly and neat, while for other kids, "clean your room" may mean get everything off the floor, stuff things in closets and throw things under the bed. One helpful recommendation for this situation is to encourage the child to take a picture of the finished product after you both agree that "the job is *done*, and *done well*." The picture is a visual reminder for next time of how the end result should look.

Here is another example of something that may resonate with parents or guardians of older teens. Many parents/guardians of children under 12 expect that everyone is home and settled by 9:00–10:00 p.m. However, just when you are ready to turn in and close down the house for the night, older teens are often getting ready to go out or to have friends drop by. When this first starts to happen, it can be quite unsettling. Since it *will* happen, parents must set ground rules about what "late" and "too late" mean. Setting expectations about this phenomenon is helpful and necessary for harmony in the home.

Disagreement over curfews is a common source of conflict between parents/guardians and teens. A parent might have a firm time in mind when deciding on a curfew but the adolescent might have a good argument about why the curfew should be extended. You can encourage the requester to present the rationale for the request. Make a good effort to listen for the logic and reasons for this petition. On the other hand, a teen might offer an excuse why this request needs to be granted. "I am the only one of my friends who has to be home by 11 on Saturday night." Being aware of these kinds of situations helps parents and guardians prepare for when they undoubtedly will occur.

There will be moments when you will have to agree to disagree with your child.

There will be moments when you will have to "agree to disagree" with your child or adolescent. This is sometimes referred to as "assessing alternatives to come to [an] agreement." This strategy may be helpful when there are strong convictions on both sides of a discussion or argument. Sometimes, taking a pause before a final decision is reached can be beneficial for all parties. The parent/guardian can decide to play the ace card of "Because I said so!" However, this seldom ends an argument and may create a barrier to reaching a mutually acceptable final agreement.

An example: Your teenage son comes home with news that he can get a great deal on a used van. "I've got the money, so you don't have to worry about it!" You know the van is in shaky condition and is not a good deal for many reasons. Your son is convinced that your reluctance is totally unreasonable. Although you may not come to a mutual agreement about the purchase of the van, you may be able to encourage your child to find a different vehicle that makes more sense in financial and safety terms. Your child may never understand your decision and you will be unlikely to change your mind, but you both can arrive at a common ground. Even though your child may be upset with you for weeks, you have decided that this outcome is acceptable for moving on.

This approach demonstrates a SEL skill related to relationship management: preventing interpersonal conflict, and managing and resolving conflicts when they occur—even when you don't agree.

Resolving Friend and Sibling Conflicts

There are many times when parents are in the role of helping resolve children's conflicts with their siblings and friends. These conflicts take many forms—every parent/guardian has dealt with one or more of the following:

1. Two preschoolers are in conflict over who gets the most Legos from the box.

2. Two 10-year-olds argue over whether the kicker in a kickball game is safe or out.

3. Two 13-year-olds shove each other after a disagreement about whose turn it is to use the skateboard.

4. Two high-school students exchange nasty text messages over the same boy they both like.

5. Two siblings fight over which show to watch on TV.

6. A child is unfairly excluded from a group activity.

In some instances, conflicts can reach the level of gang violence. For purposes of this book, we will talk about the types of conflicts that are typically resolved by parents or guardians.

As parents, none of us likes resolving conflicts that involve our children. However, these conflicts are often inevitable. The protocol below is designed to help parents resolve conflicts in ways that also develop the SEL skills of the antagonists. Using the protocol below (or a similar structure) teaches children and adolescents to understand their feelings and those of others, and, more important, to resolve conflicts in ways that are learning experiences for all. This protocol is designed to have a parent/guardian act as the facilitator. However, it can eventually be used by "peer facilitators," as is often done in middle and high schools.

Ending the conflict and resolving the conflict are two very different processes.

Ending the conflict and *resolving the conflict* are two very different processes. Ending the conflict typically makes everyone safe by stopping the behavior that is physically, emotionally, or interpersonally detrimental. However, ending the conflict does not resolve the conflict. Resolving the conflict requires getting to its root with the antagonists and resolving the root cause. Simply ending conflicts between children improves their present situation but rarely has a positive impact on their skills of understanding and resolving conflicts.

It is during the resolution of the conflict that social-emotional learning takes place. The first decision we must make in resolving the conflict is when is the best time to approach it. Sometimes, the intensity of the conflict is so high that the best time to resolve it is not immediately afterwards. Some "cooling off" time may be needed before we take steps to resolving the dispute.

Most resolutions consist of some form of **conflict-resolution discussion**. This discussion includes the two antagonists and someone who facilitates the resolution. Below is a protocol for resolving a conflict between two people. It is important to note that no single series of fixed steps is an exact way to resolve every conflict. We offer the following as a template to begin planning facilitating such a discussion.

Conflict-Resolution Protocol

Step 1: Explaining the Rules

The parent or guardian who facilitates the conflict resolution begins by explaining the steps that the discussion will follow (e.g., who will speak first). He/she also provides some ground rules if necessary and explains the objective of the conference. Ground rules can include:

1. Speak in a calm voice
2. Don't interrupt another speaker (you will get your turn to speak)
3. No name-calling
4. Listen to the speaker

Step 2: Deciding Who Talks First

A decision that the parent/guardian facilitator makes after framing the rules is whether the facilitator shares what he/she knows about the conflict first, or if the antagonists go first by each in turn stating their side of the story. The advantage of having the antagonists go first is that they each feel "heard" before the facilitator says too much. The advantage of having the facilitator go first is that the information may compel the antagonists to be more truthful.

Another strategy is telling the parties you have gathered information about the issue but want to give them the first opportunity to talk. Knowing you have information may dissuade them from fabrications, since they do not know what you know and will likely not want to be caught in a lie. Your decision of the best way to start also depends on what you know about the personalities of those involved.

Once all the information is out in the open, the facilitator frames the issue by explaining what he/she sees as the reason for the conflict, and which issues need be addressed in order to resolve it.

Step 3: Make Sure You Are Objective

If you are the facilitator resolving a conflict between two or more of your own children, you are likely going to be objective in your interactions. However, if you are resolving a conflict between your child and another child, *it is essential to force yourself to be objective.* That is not as easy as it may seem. We all have the "mama/papa bear" in us that wants to defend our child, thus making it difficult for us to be objective about our own child's role in the conflict. It doesn't mean we can't be objective. It does mean we will need to make an extra effort to be objective. It helps to remind yourself that defending your child will be less helpful to his/her long-term development than resolving the conflict objectively will be.

Step 4: Gathering Information

Prior to the conference, it is important to gather as much information as possible about the conflict. Some information will come from the antagonists, other details come from witnesses and other sources (e.g., other players or viewers of the game), and some originate from your own observations of the interactions leading up to the conflict (e.g., reading the offending text messages, etc.). Sometimes this will enable the facilitator to discover additional information that may help resolve the conflict. Once as much information as possible is gathered, the parent/guardian can begin to consider the situation and get ready with questions or comments to help resolve the issue.

Step 5: Presentation and Response

Each antagonist is asked to describe the issue as honestly and clearly as possible. During his/her *presentation*, the facilitator is ensuring that the speaker gets to make his/her case without interruption. After the presentation, the facilitator may also ask questions to gather additional information or to clarify a point. Once the first party is finished and the issue is on the table, the other party explains his/her point of view in the *response* stage. Managing this stage well by responding calmly and professionally is essential to preventing the meeting from degenerating into an argument.

At this point, conflicting views or events are often introduced into the discussion. The parties will be tempted to vigorously defend their own view and cast aspersions on the other's. A firm repeat of the rules by the facilitator and an assurance that everyone will have adequate time to speak is important. The facilitator must enable each speaker to tell his or her side without being interrupted. After the response, the facilitator may ask questions to gather additional information or to clarify a point.

Step 6: Creating Common Understanding

The parent/guardian facilitator asks each party to restate the *other* party's position in a way that shows he/she heard and understood the issue from the perspective of the other. In some circumstances, the facilitator may believe that restating what the other said will be counter-productive—for example, if the facilitator believes that the presentations will be interrupted and may lead to a renewed argument. In this instance, the facilitator can restate what has been said by both parties. Before moving to the next step, the facilitator ensures that all the information has been stated and that each party's position has been understood by all.

Step 7: Generating Solutions

The facilitating parent/guardian opens the discussion to both parties to begin suggesting possible solutions. The facilitator asks questions that help the parties come to a solution. As ideas are expressed, the facilitator may repeat or paraphrase to ensure that everyone has the same understanding. The facilitator may also suggest solutions.

There are some cases in which both sides are being stubborn and are not willing to compromise at the outset. In those circumstances, it can be helpful to explain the alternative to coming to agreement. For example: "If you both can't agree on what show to watch, then the TV will stay off until we get a solution." Or, "If you cannot come up with a plan for who gets to use my subway pass on Saturday night, then you will each have to pay your own subway fares."

Best options. Once some possible solutions are on the table, the participants usually begin to feel less tense and can discuss the solutions, working toward consensus on the one that will work best. This is important practice for developing both relationship skills, such as evaluating others' emotional reactions to varied situations, and respect for others, by listening carefully, accurately, and objectively.

At the end of this stage, an agreement is established. In some circumstances, it may be helpful to write down the solution. It is important to restate the agreement and have all parties agree to the resolution before the meeting ends. In circumstances pertaining to a recurring problem (e.g., how we resolve who gets to choose the TV show), it is important to have the agreement written-up and distributed to all parties as soon as is practicable. The more time that passes between incidents, the greater the likelihood that recollections of what was agreed upon will "evolve" or one party may change his or her mind.

Step 8: Ending the Discussion

At the end of the discussion, it is important for the guardian/parent facilitator to bring closure by thanking all parties and dispersing them promptly. The end of the meeting is often called "the danger zone:" As participants relax and think the ground rules have ended, there is a high likelihood that someone will misinterpret what was said or begin to revisit the issue. When this occurs, the meeting can quickly circle back to the presentation and response stages. The hostility returns and the participants are likely to distrust the outcome of the meeting.

The longer the meeting stays in the danger zone, the more difficult it becomes to implement a solution." When dealing with siblings, it is not always possible to put an end to their being together after the meeting. For example, if they are siblings who share a bedroom or if you are on two-hour car trip, then there is no option but to have them remain together. In these circumstances, if the parent/guardian believes that the solution reached is the *best* solution, it might need to be "enforced" by reminding the children of the less-than-optimal alternatives to following through on what they agreed to. At this point, it may even include a consequence, since one party is going back on his or her earlier agreement.

Step 9: Follow-Up

It is important that the facilitator ensures that what was agreed upon is, in fact, implemented. Every solution requires a certain level of compromise by both parties. Each party has probably agreed to one or more things that they were (or are) reluctant to do. This reluctance may cause them unconsciously (or consciously) to delay following through on what was agreed to. Lack of timely follow-through will result in the quick resurfacing of the tension between the parties and is likely to undermine the agreement.

Reducing the Parent's or Guardian's Role

Under circumstances in which the antagonists have regular conflicts with one another, it might eventually become possible for the facilitator to take a declining role. For example, once the protocol has been used a few times, the facilitator chooses to participate in steps one to six, eight, and nine. The antagonists may be able to do step seven (generating solutions and choosing the best option). As time goes on, the facilitator may be able to reduce his/her role more.

A long-term goal is that antagonists start to recognize conflicts at the outset and use some form of the conflict-resolution protocol on their own. You may remember the twin brothers in Chapter 1 who were in the "punishment room" and left to create a solution as to who would ride "shotgun" in the car. The parent/guardian facilitator required that the brothers remain in the room alone until they reached a resolution. This worked because the parent had clearly done a very good job of laying out the ground rules, which insured that generating a solution didn't result in a verbal or physical fight.

Conflict-Resolution Summary

Important relationships with adults (parents/guardians and other adults in a child or adolescent's life) play an essential role in developing social-emotional learning.

Important relationships with adults (parents, guardians, and other adults in a child's life) play an essential role in developing social-emotional skills. Table 3.1 gives an overview of connections between SEL skills and the questions used in the conflict-resolution protocol. These skills are developed through interactions with peers and important adults. Developing the SEL skills to build positive relationships with peers also varies greatly among people; some people have more interpersonal skills than others. Whatever the participants' skill levels in developing interpersonal relationships, parents/guardians can further their youngsters' skills and improve their self-awareness, self-management, relationship skills, social awareness, and responsible interpersonal decision-making.

What if it doesn't work and the problem is not resolved? Even in circumstances where the antagonists cannot agree on the solution, important social and emotional learning taking place. Don't be discouraged, and continue to use the process as issues arise. The modeling they are exposed to in the process will be beneficial to their long-term ability to resolve conflicts.

Consequences vs. Punishment

Some characteristics of **punishments** are that they:
- Have an angry tone
- Are not related to the behavior
- Leave the child feeling she or he is the problem, rather than his or her *behavior*
- Use fear as an external motivator for stopping the behavior
- Leave the child feeling shamed

Table 3.1 Self-Awareness and Social Awareness and the Conflict-Resolution Protocol

Behavior	Questions that Supporting the Development of SEL Skills
Self-Awareness	
Label and recognize their own and others' emotions	• How did it make you feel when he called you that name? • Why do you think he called you that name? • Why did you call him that name?
Analyze emotions and how they affect others	• How do you think he felt when you called him that name? • Did you want to make him feel that way? Why? • What do you think you might do differently in a similar situation next time?
Social-Awareness	
Listen closely and accurately	• Were you able to listen closely, and accurately retell the other person's story? • If the other person disagreed with your version of the story, were you able to understand why there was disagreement?
Look at things from others' points of view	• Did the other person understand your point of view? • Did you understand his or her perspective?
Respect others' feelings and reactions	• Were you able to stay calm throughout the meeting? • If the other person was upset or angry, were you able to respect those emotions—or not react to them?

Consequences, on the other hand, are assigned as follows:

• In a calm and matter-of-fact voice
• Are a logical outcome of the behavior
• Help the child understand the negative impact of the behavior on himself/herself and others
• Leave the child believing the behavior is the problem (not himself or herself)
• Build an intrinsic desire to use more appropriate behaviors

Example: A child "borrows" something from a sibling without asking, and loses the item. A *punishment* might be to scold the child for his/her irresponsibility, "You always lose things!" As to *consequences*, in addition to having the child offer an apology, you might also ground him/her for a week, have the child pay for the lost item out of his/her own money, or find a way to replace the missing object.

A more serious example: An adolescent is arrested for shoplifting and the court assigns a punishment of community service—cleaning up trash with a crew on the side of the highway. The parent/guardian may not think the teen will truly grasp the seriousness of his/her offense through this type of punishment, and therefore works with the court to come up with a more meaningful way of making restitution. For example, the teen must volunteer at a homeless shelter where he/she is exposed to those who are truly in need of life's basic necessities.

Consequences are often more compelling in teaching the SEL skill of responsible decision-making." Punishment may provide an immediate solution to an infraction, but a consequence is likely to stay longer with the child.

Conclusion

After a serious discussion with a child or adolescent, parents and guardians must be prepared to revisit some of the points made at the end of the conversation. It might go something like this:

"So, Jose, after our talk we agreed that the following things will happen. You will make sure to fill the car up with gas if you are the last one who drives it. I will also return that same courtesy to you. As long as you keep doing this and demonstrate that you will be responsible about this, you should be able to use the car when it is available. Now, please tell me your understanding of our agreement."

Or, like this:

"So, Timmy. This morning was very chaotic! You had to run all over the house to find your homework and backpack. What is your plan for getting organized for tomorrow? Let's keep track of how you do with this over the next week and then we can check back in to see how things are going."

Raising children who are socially and emotionally competent is always a work-in-progress. As parents and guardians, we must also recognize how we can improve in this area; it is an ongoing process for us, too. Admitting to your child that you made a mistake about something and apologizing about it is a powerful and important lesson.

Discussion Questions

1. Chapter 3 focuses on resolving conflicts and other important conversations that you have with your child. Select a passage that resonates with you and relate it to a situation that you have experienced.

2. Your son arrives home from school and goes straight up to his room, saying very little. Something seems to be bothering him, and you want to encourage him to confide in you. Using some of the strategies mentioned in this chapter, what approach could you take to engage him in conversation?

3. What are some strategies that a parent or guardian can utilize to turn an unconscious competence into a conscious competence?

4. After reviewing the difference between suggestion recommendations and direction recommendations, discuss a situation in which you would use each.

5. Imagine the following scenario: your child is having trouble getting up for school. It is becoming a source of frustration and friction between you and your child. Using descriptive feedback, how might you initiate a discussion about this situation?

6. There are times when you and your child may struggle to agree on a decision, e.g., curfew, purchasing a phone, his or her friends, etc. How can assessing alternatives to coming to an agreement assist in negotiating a resolution to this scenario?

7. What are the important differences between "ending the conflict" and "resolving the conflict?"

References

Pollock, W., *Real Boys—Rescuing Our Sons from the Myth of Boyhood.* New York: Owl Books, Henry Holt and Company, 1999.

Ribas, W., Brady, D., Tamerat, J., Deane, J., Billings, C., Greer, V. *Instructional Practices That Maximize Student Achievement, For Teachers, By Teachers.* Norwood, MA: Ribas Publications, Inc., 2017.

4

How Questions Encourage Higher-Order Thinking and Deep Conversations about Social-Emotional Skills

Life's Questions:
What Do You Say When…?

Throughout a child's life, parents and guardians support their child's social-emotional growth in five categories of social-emotional (SEL) skills. The categories encompass a child's understanding of him- or herself, of others, and how to solve personal problems, such as:

- (**Self-Management**) Your toddler just melted down in the middle of the grocery store.

- (**Self-Awareness**) Your middle-schooler brought home her first C with a comment that she does not participate in class.

- (**Relationship Skills**) Your high school freshman has brought home his new friends and you're not sure they're good influences.

- (**Social Awareness**) Your seventh grader seems to spend all her time on social media.

- (**Responsible Decision-Making**) Your third grader has found out about homelessness and wants to do something to help.

Five Essential Social-Emotional Conversations

In this chapter, we use questions aligned to the five SEL skills—**self-awareness, self-management, social awareness, relationship skills,** and **responsible decision-making**—to help focus important conversations that parents and guardians have with their children. The list of key questions below includes related questions that also need to be addressed throughout a child's life.

At times, you might ask these questions directly, while in other instances the questions might be part of a longer conversation. These talks with your child may be easygoing and brief—"How do you like the team?"—or longer and more intense when they are about ongoing concerns. The conversations may take place while driving your child to a soccer game, while playing a board game with your preschooler, or in a quiet, private place.

As children grow to adulthood, the five questions remain relevant and essential but the approach may change based upon the child's age, concerns, or the need to discuss a specific issue. For example, when considering the SEL skill of **self-awareness**, we must understand our own strengths and weaknesses in order to think through the day's events or solve a specific problem effectively. For the SEL skill of **self-management**, you may recognize and encourage your preschooler's need to dress himself independently. Years later, the same child may might need to develop consistency in cleaning her room or independence when applying for a summer job. In young adulthood, the child's focus may be on setting priorities every day so she can be ready for school, work, and soccer. At each age, children need to work on all the SEL skills. The above example shows how the specific context evolves from getting dressed to cleaning her room to setting priorities.

Key Social-Emotional Questions

Self-Awareness
Who are you?
- Does your child know his strengths and weaknesses?
- Can your child describe how she feels?
- Does your child feel his efforts are effective?
- Does she have a growth mindset and believe that she can improve her skills?

Self-Management
How do your actions reflect who you are?
- Can your child manage her impulses?
- How does your child manage stress?
- Is your child engaged and motivated in his life?
- Is your child organized?

Social Awareness
How effectively do you relate to others?
- Does your child have empathy for others?
- Does your child respect the diversity of others in the world?
- Does your child respect others' values and ideas even if they're different from his or her own values or ideas?

Relationship Management

How effectively do you work and play along with others?

- Does your child get along with her friends?
- Does your child like to go to social events?
- Does your child participate effectively on a team or in a group?

Responsible Decision-Making

How do you solve problems in ways that reflect your values and beliefs?

- Can your child solve problems?
- Does your child have principles or a code of ethics that she uses to solve problems?

These skills often overlap in everyday life, although the following section addresses each separately.

Consider Yourself a Life Coach

According to Jenny Rogers, parental coaching is a key component of providing appropriate support for children's growth (*Coaching Skills*, 2012). Parental coaching encompasses a lifetime of conversations with your child about feelings, friends, and concerns. Instead of focusing on technique, as in sports, life coaching is a process in which parents help their children think through their problems. With their guardian's or parent's coaching, children improve their SEL skills, gain insight, and resolve their social-emotional problems. Rogers emphasizes that the parent should avoid solving the problem for their child, but instead should slow down the interaction and use questions to evoke deliberation about workable solutions in the child.

As a child's life coach, parents and guardians become involved in deep conversations with the child.

Instead of saying, "Tell him to give you the football now—and tell him I said so!" and thereby solving the child's problem, Rogers recommends that parents and guardians take the stance of a coach and say instead, "Why do you think he won't let you have the football? And what started this? So, what do you think he really wants? … What's your plan?"

By using this kind of child-focused response, the parent places the responsibility of solving problems into the hands of the child and puts the child into the position of agent and problem-solver. The resulting conversation helps the child see patterns in his behavior and he can begin to work on changing those patterns.

When adult intervention is removed as the solution to problems, the parent demonstrates that the child is a competent problem-solver. Of course, at times parental or guardian intervention is the only reasonable choice—for example, when the child cannot reasonably resolve the situation on her own due to her age or because the situation is too complex.

Bringing the Essential Skills Together: Reflection, Metacognition, and Other Higher-Order Thinking

As their children's life coach, parents and guardians often become involved in deep and meaningful conversations with the children. These conversations require the support of a knowledgeable and supportive adult who can help their child think more deeply and thus learn to use two of the higher-order thinking skills, reflection and metacognition.

Reflection—looking back on the past—helps a child remember what she has done and consider its consequences. For example: "When I was upset, I just walked away." **Metacognition** helps a child gain insight into the patterns in his thinking or behavior. For example: "Every time I get angry when Jill says something I don't like, I just leave." In this case, the child understands that she generally avoids expressing her anger and leaves upset. By seeing her pattern of avoiding confrontation through metacognition, she can decide, perhaps with a parent's help, to face her friend and tell the friend that her words are upsetting her. Getting to this level of metacognition may take a few conversations that provide the child with alternatives and specific ways to express her feelings.

To support a child's metacognition and reflection, and to teach him/her to **self-monitor**, **self-assess**, and **self-regulate**, requires many thoughtful conversations between parent and child. Reflection and metacognition help your child see the patterns and consequences of his/her behavior. These skills are essential for children's growth and development; children need the insight and assistance of an adult who understands the importance of SEL skills and children's needs to understand their identities, emotions, and behaviors.

Reflection and metacognition work in tandem. When a child monitors her own behavior through reflection, she begins to see patterns in her own or others' behavior. That is, she begins to have a "metacognitive" awareness of behavior patterns. For example, the child may begin to see that whenever she is called on in class, she feels uncomfortable. As she begins to understand how this emotion is triggered, she is taking her first step in metacognition. Once she sees a pattern, she will be more able to recognize and then solve a problem independently. For example, the child may decide that she will answer when she is called on because she now realizes that every time she makes herself answer, she feels less uncomfortable. She has recognized a pattern. In addition, she is learning to use reflection and metacognition for self-monitoring and self-assessing her progress. As she begins to see that her actions can result in positive changes in her life, she will develop a stronger sense of being a problem-solver. She may come home one day and say, "Mom, I raised my hand today and answered a question." The mother might say, "Tell me more. What happened?" As this conversation unfolds, by recognizing progress and strategizing next steps, she is developing a "growth mindset" about school participation and her capacity to change her behavior. Developing metacognition helps the child see that she is instrumental in her own development.

With a growth mindset, a child can see herself as a competent problem-solver who can change.

The essence of having a growth mindset is believing that through your action, you can change and grow. Without this belief, the above child might have a "fixed mindset" and believe she has no power to affect a negative situation and will be forever uncomfortable when she's called on in class. With a fixed mindset, she'd believe she was born shy or introverted and can do nothing about it. With a growth mindset, a child can see herself as a competent problem-solver who can change.

Reflecting, metacognition, and problem-solving often require the support of a parent-as-coach. Jennifer Kolari, a Toronto therapist and author of *Connected Parenting: How to Raise a Great Kid*, says:

It's our job as parents and guardians to help our kids sort through and process the things that happen to them during the day. 'They don't have the higher-order thinking to do it on their own yet,' she says.

You may not hear about every single triumph or trial, but these ideas [about talking to your child] can get your kids to open up to you at every age (2010, p. 5).

Metacognition, Reflection, and Analysis

Metacognition, reflection, and analysis are higher-order thinking skills. In Table 4.1, three levels of thinking are defined with examples. **Recall** is lower-order thinking, an essential thinking skill that requires remembering something—an event, a story, or an idea. **Comprehension** is a more complex thinking skill. With comprehension, events, stories, and ideas are both remembered *and* understood. At the **higher-order level**, thinking is most complex and may include reflection or analysis. In the table, the questions below each term require progressively more complex thinking in two situations: the first about a visit to an aquarium, the second about a new year in school. Moving from left to right, the questions become more challenging and require deeper and deeper thinking.

Table 4.1 Lower and Higher-order Thinking Examples

Recall *Remembering*	Comprehension *Understanding*	Higher-Order *Reflecting, Analyzing, Creating Solutions*
What happened when we went to the aquarium?	You told me a shark can never stop swimming. Why?	So even though a shark may be something we stay away from when we're swimming in the ocean, why are they a necessary part of the ocean?
Tell me about your new classes this term.	Which course do you think will be your favorite?	Your progress report shows you're getting all B's this term, but one comment says you haven't turned in some work. What's going on this year?

Talking It Out

Why are these questions and conversations so important? Why do we want to get kids talking? Talk is an essential part of learning deeply; talk can solidify learning. At the first level, we all have a voice "talking" in our heads—our inner voice. When we hear or read a new idea, we begin to understand it. However, until we can talk about the idea using our own words in conversation, and then apply that understanding to a new situation, the concept or idea is not deeply understood. Therefore, knowledge is deepened through talk and application in varied situations.

Talk is an essential part of learning deeply; talk can solidify learning.

For example, your child may have difficulty playing with his peers because he is unwilling to share. You may see that he often leaves the group of children and comes home looking angry. He may be aware that he's angry about what happened as he played but he may not understand that he can solve the problem if he changes his behavior and learns to share. The first step in the conversation would be to help him become aware that he needs to learn to share if he wants to play with others. You might ask, "What happened just before you left your friends?" You are asking what he was thinking as he was asked to share.

Your question, "So, tell me why did you leave Tom and Joey? You looked upset," is meant to trigger the realization (metacognition) that his own thinking ('I'm not sharing this toy') and behavior is probably the reason he's not happy—and that he might be able to resolve this problem if he changes his thinking and behavior.

At this point, as his coach, you need to help him understand the *social* reason for sharing in order to get along with others. You might have to role-play to help him learn how to share. You could pretend to be a playmate who wants a turn and you and your child might try to solve the problem together. You might say, "But you have played with that all morning, it's my turn now," and work with your child to come up with a way of responding that is different from running away, and a way of sharing without feeling it is unfair.

Helping your child understand why sharing and taking turns is an important social skill. By encouraging him to practice the skill, and helping him to change his behavior, you have supported his increasing social-emotional skills.

The above conversation progressed from lower-order thinking all the way to metacognition. It began as the child identified and named the situation (not sharing) that caused him to unhappily leave his friends. The talk then progressed to a higher-level skill—an understanding of the social purpose of sharing. Finally, when the child recognized that his pattern of running away is what made him unhappy—a metacognition—he began to change his behavior. Ultimately, through working as a coach, the parent helped the child understand that he can solve his own problems.

Growth Mindset

The essential conversations about social-emotional issues support a growth mindset, the belief that over time a child can improve social-emotional skills and solve their social-emotional problems. Initially, a child may need your support, but over time he/she will learn to use these skills independently. We all have both fixed and growth mindsets about various aspects of our lives. We can believe that we *can't* improve in some areas, such as making friends, and believe that we *can* improve in others, such as learning how to participate on a team. For years, psychologists believed that intelligence was fixed, and schools placed students in leveled classrooms, assuming that their intelligence level could not grow. Now they understand there is room for growth and that a challenging classroom is generally the best environment for all students to learn.

Creating the Space and Time for Conversation

In my experience raising sons and daughters, I found that my sons often answered my, "So how was school?" with monosyllables: "Good" or "OK" or "All right." In contrast, my daughter often gave me the rundown and all the nuances about her friends, teachers, and feelings. For my daughter, I just needed to make sure we had enough time to talk and that I listened with my full attention. However, with my sons I needed to find ways to make talking more comfortable and possible.

To do this, start with an open mind and consider changing the timing. Wait until the emotion of the moment has gone and you feel ready to thoroughly discuss a situation as a listener *and* a questioner. In addition, you can change the question. The question does not have to be directly stated, but rather can be embedded in the conversation. The question could be neutral and not connected to your child. "What do you think about having assigned chores?" To determine the tone you're setting, you can try the "stance test."

The "Stance" Test

Having a nonjudgmental or neutral stance takes work on the parent's part. Sometimes when it's difficult to get your child to listen, part of the problem might be the emotions or the position—stance—that you express. (This might be unconscious on your part.) To determine if your stance fits the conversation, you can try this simple test: put yourself in your child's shoes. Imagine being about to have a conversation with someone who has authority over you—your supervisor or a person whom you see as powerful. As this person is about to talk to you, how do you feel? Are you worried that you might lose your job? Are you embarrassed just to have this conversation? Take that feeling, then imagine that the powerful person who is starting the conversation is *you*.

Child not doing a chore: My son has neglected to take out the garbage for the fifth time this year. I want to say, "How can you forget to take out the garbage again? I don't expect much of you, just this, and yet you NEVER accomplish it." Apply the "stance test" solution.

You're not doing your job: Now imagine your boss comes to you and says in an angry and loud voice, "How could you let us down again? This is what you always do." How would you feel? You'd probably feel as if you were about to be fired and that you were a colossal failure. Unfortunately, these comments probably won't inspire you to make positive changes. Instead you might just want to disappear or to itemize everything negative you can think of about the boss and the company.

Finding the Right Tone

With my children, I learned to avoid becoming a member of the Inquisition. I found that even if I had a burning question or concern, I needed to wait for the right time for the conversation. Sometimes that meant after a child had gone out to play with friends or had a chance to call a friend, have a snack, or simply relax. Sometimes, after one of my sons had done homework, watched his favorite show, and texted friends, he would be accessible and tell me he was unhappy with school, and that he had counted how many times Miss Murphy yelled that day. "Did she yell at you?" "Me? No. I just do my work and wait for the end of the day." This answer sent me to the principal to seek his support.

I learned to keep my tone positive and never to begin with a question that could be interpreted as "the third degree" of questioning. I tried to be casual. As an entrée, books and stories about my own experiences often led to meaningful discussions.

With all my children, I learned to avoid becoming a member of the Inquisition.

Remember that parents' and guardians' responses to children's behaviors can at times be colored by the belief that this action is larger than a single instance. They may think the single act symbolizes an intolerable trait, such as defiance, forgetfulness, or lack of consideration for others, in their child. If the parent can neutralize this perception and see the behavior as something that needs to be unlearned—and not an act of defiance, etc.—then the conversation will be more positive and can reach a better resolution.

Avoiding the Judgmental

To have deep conversations that support your child's insight about himself, you need to create a "safe space" for conversations that might at times address a child's most sensitive issues. A safe space reflects your supportive, caring attitude, and avoids anyone taking a judgmental attitude. As you may have experienced, even the mere mention of a subject—a messy room or being late—can trigger emotional outbursts and arguments. To create a space for reasonable conversation, a parent must deliberately create a safe space or wait for a time when emotions are less intense.

Judgmental question: "Lucy, how many times have I told you to pick up your toys and put your dirty clothes in the hamper?"

Nonjudgmental space and time: The parent waits until she is no longer irritated with her child. She finds a book about clean rooms or messy ones, perhaps a humorous one such as *The Plant That Ate Dirty Socks* by Nancy R. McArthur, and shares it with her daughter at bedtime. At some point while laughing and talking about the book, the mother can breach the subject, perhaps indirectly: "Lucy, it looks like messy rooms happen to lots of kids."

At a later age, the nonjudgmental stance continues to be important:

Judgmental: "Julie, you have been late twice this week. You are defying the rules of this house. I'm taking away the car for the next week."

Nonjudgmental: Julie, what happened last night?

According to some psychologists, parents and guardians sometimes wrongly perceive children's behaviors as moral choices and then may make a harsh judgment about a child's action. For example, if the child doesn't clean his room, a parent may think this means the child is lazy; if the child comes home late, a parent may believe this is an act of defiance. Some psychologists suggest a neutral attitude can facilitate a deeper conversation and avoid a reprimand and punishment. Jessica Minahan suggests that we ought to look at misbehavior as yet-to-be-developed skills (2012, p. 317). By suspending judgment—and the feeling of betrayal or anger that often accompanies it—a parent's attitude can signal to the child that he/she is not "in trouble," that this will not lead to an argument, and that discussion is possible. The focus of the conversation can then shift to solving the problem *with* the child and helping the child to develop an important life skill.

Having a positive parent-child relationship is the key to having meaningful conversations between parent and child. Even before words are used, parents and guardians begin building a positive relationship in a child's life as they respond to the child's early expressions and words. The first smile is as delightful as the first words of "Mmmmum" or "Daaaa" or "Up?" Parents must listen and attend to a child's emotions, words, and behavior from the very beginning.

Authentic Listening

Although we hear others' words, frequently we're not really listening but thinking about what to say next.

Although we *hear* the words of others, frequently we're not really listening but, instead, are thinking about what we are going to say next. However, to be effective, communication requires two-way *listening* as well as two-way *talking*. Responsive and respectful listening can set a positive tone.

The Safe Haven of Books, Movies, and Games

In parents' and guardians' and their children's busy and frequently stressful days, it is necessary to establish daily activities that are safe for relaxing and, ideally, for conversation. Everyday activities, such as mealtimes, car rides to and from school or grandma's, sporting events, or even grocery shopping, can become opportunities for spontaneous conversations. Other possibilities depend on your child's age and interests, but sharing books and movies, playing board games or working on a family puzzle, practicing a sport, or even shopping at the mall can create an atmosphere for conversation. I found that driving in the car with my three sons (when I turned down the music) sometimes resulted in memorable and meaningful conversations.

Books and Read-Alouds

Besides evoking emotion, stories can activate parts in the brain so that the listener turns the story into their own idea. In a process called "neural coupling," the brain mirrors the emotions of the story-teller and releases dopamine (see Chapter 5), making the story itself easier to remember. The most effective stories can compel change and growth in the reader or listener. They engage us when we can identify with the storyteller or the main character of the story. They evoke emotion, generate energy, and can encourage us to change our thinking and behavior.

Some of my favorite resources are books. According to recent research, when read for pleasure, books, and even poetry, are more memorable than mere facts. Plus, stories can make us more human because they support and teach empathy toward others. In Derek Beres's article, "How Reading Rewires Your Brain for More Intelligence and Empathy," he recounts that reading increases intelligence, improves communication, and lets us "practice being human" (Beres 2017, p. 2). Readers not only discover others' ideas and perspectives, they experience the emotions of the storyteller. Accordingly, when children read, they become better readers and, as important for their social-emotional growth, develop the emotional intelligence that helps them make better decisions, develop better relationships,develop compassion, and understand themselves, their behaviors, and their friends more deeply.

Books, including picture books, can provide a neutral space from which to begin a discussion.

Through the imaginative process that reading involves, children have the opportunity to do what they often cannot do in real life—become thoroughly involved in the inner lives of others, better understand them, and eventually become more aware of themselves (Shechtman, 2009, *Treating Child and Adolescent Aggression Through Bibliotherapy*).

Unlike lectures, memorizing facts, or reading to prepare for a test, reading and sharing stories engage us deeply.

Unlike lectures, memorizing facts, or reading to prepare for a test, reading and sharing stories engage us deeply. Brain research verifies that this is true. When a reader, listener, or moviegoer is attentive and experiencing a story or movie, not only are the logical and language processing areas of our brain activated, but also all the other areas in the brain that would have been activated if we had actually experienced the story.

One of my favorite books is *Where the Wild Things Are*, by Maurice Sendak, which I've read with my children and grandchildren. The book is fun to read and its message creates a reassuring and safe space for children. Through Max's adventures with the wild things, Sendak's book shows kids that they, too, can have wild episodes of being "bad," but their need for the sustenance of the family (and a dinner that is still warm) brings them back to family where they are safe and cared for.

The reader is shocked as Max dons his wolf suit, wreaks havoc at home, and then is sent to bed without any supper as his punishment. Max imagines he leaves his bedroom to dance a wild dance with a whole island of wild things. He subdues these creatures and becomes their king. However, he doesn't want to stay on this wild island because he begins to feel lonely. He decides to return home where he finds a warm dinner. The story arc takes us along with Max being out of control, running away, subduing wild emotions, feeling lonely, and finally feeling loved despite his transgressions. As readers, my children and grandchildren experienced the same emotions. The story tells children that even if they are "bad," they are always loved. Each time I read this book, I love it more for its message that all children can have wild impulses and, at times, act on them, but that home is there to welcome them back.

Reading books lets your child see others' lives, different perspectives, and others' problems to solve. At the end of this chapter, there is a list of books, movies, and activities that are matched with specific skills, along with links to more resources.

Shopping, Driving to School, and the Movies

For my daughter and me, shopping was always good for a day-long discussion about her friends, concerns, and successes. And, at a time when two of my sons' trip to school took an hour, we'd listen to a story and chat about the problems and characters. I remember taking two of my children to see the movie *Charlotte's Web* and asking them, as I generally did, "What was your favorite part of the movie?" On this day, I was greeted with total silence. Soon I realized there was sniffling, not silence, in the back seat.

Finally my daughter was able to say, "It was too sad."
"Why so sad, Liv?"
"Charlotte died."
"That's true. That was sad. The movie tried to make you feel better, though, at the end."
"Yeah, her babies were born. But I loved Charlotte, and she was gone."
(More tears.)

The movie and conversation created an unanticipated opportunity to discuss the loss of someone (or something) we care about and to acknowledge how sad it makes us feel. It also let my children consider how well the movie solved the problem—or didn't, since Charlotte was gone forever—and what this meant to them. It triggered a long conversation about how sad they felt when Pippin, their English sheep dog, was hit by a car and died, how there would never be another Pippin ... though they really do like their new dog, Brigit, but Brigit isn't as funny and doesn't herd them as Pippin did, since she was an Old English sheepherding dog ...

The Many Types of Questions

Parents and guardians ask many questions of their children every day. The four major purposes of these questions are listed in Figure 4.1, with both an early childhood question and a question for older children for each question type. Questions are important for:

- understanding the child's thinking
- connecting to the child's interests or memories
- helping your child reflect on his/her thinking and behavior
- engaging a child in an activity

Figure 4.1 The Four Main Types of Parental Questions

To more deeply understand the child's thinking:
- You are very quiet today. Are you thinking about something serious?
- How's field hockey going?

To engage a child in an activity:
- Have you seen the new crayons on the table?
- Do you want to play catch?

To connect with a child's interests or memories:
- Remember when we went to the zoo?
- Who's working on the social justice project with you?

To help children consider and reflect upon their thinking and actions:
- Why did you decide to invite the new boy in your class to play time?
- When did you decide you wanted a part-time job?

Using Questions to Encourage SEL Development with Your Child

In each of the following sections, we look individually at the five social-emotional skills.

Each section includes:

* The principal areas for support in a child's development
* Questions you can ask yourself and your child
* Activities for various stages that can support deep, engaging discussions are labeled with their applicable age group:

  Y = early childhood up to kindergarten

  E = elementary grades (1–6)

  YA = adolescence and young adult

Self-Awareness

Principal areas for support in a child's development of self-awareness

Parents and guardians need to help children become more effectively self-aware so they become more conscious of what is going on in their own thinking, values, and emotions.

Questions you can ask yourself and your child (perhaps indirectly) to support the child's growth in self-awareness

Recognizing emotions

Y: How do you feel at the end of *Charlotte's Web*?

E: How does being successful in geometry make you feel?

YA: When you heard about the robbery, how did you feel?

Understanding thoughts

Y: What were you thinking when you gave Dad the card you made for him?

E: What do you think Max was thinking when he sailed away from his home?

YA: What are you thinking about moving to a new school?

Understanding how your emotions and thoughts influence your actions

Y: When you stormed out of the room, what were you thinking?

E: When you decided to leave the course, how did you feel?

YA: What were you thinking when you didn't reply to my text?

Understanding your strengths and weaknesses

Y: What's the most challenging position on the team for you?

E: When all your friends are smoking, what do you do?

YA: How can you balance school with your new job?

Understanding the need for a positive, confident attitude, and a growth mindset

Y: How long did it take you to solve that puzzle with your friends?

E: Can you tell me how hard you've been practicing for the school play?

YA: When you saw the shocking Instagram photos with your friends, what did you do?

Activities that support deep, engaging discussions about self-awareness

Y: Draw a picture of yourself.

Y: Draw faces with at least three different emotions. Label the emotions.

E: Draw a picture of yourself and tell a story with you in it.

E: Draw your own expressions while you think about three characters from the movie. Explain why you feel this way.

YA: In your project, "Be the Change You Wish to See in the World," what problem did you look at? Anorexia? Opioids? Tell me what you found out.

YA: Share a shocking neighborhood story or something from social-media with your child and ask him or her how they would have responded.

Table 4.2 Summary of Self-Awareness Skills

Self-Awareness Skill	SEL Behaviors	SEL Activities
Self-awareness is the ability to accurately recognize one's own emotions, thoughts, and values, and how they influence behavior. The skill includes the ability to accurately assess one's strengths and limitations, with a well-grounded sense of confidence, optimism, and a "growth mindset."	• Identifying emotions • Accurate self-perception • Recognizing strengths • Self-confidence • Self-efficacy	**Questions** • What emotion is this? • What does happy look like? Sad? Confused? **Activities** • Read a shared book, blog, or magazine • Create a selfie book • Create a book about Me • Keep a diary that you write together • Create an "I can" box, with notes for each success • Set goals and keep charts on child's wall • Make an "I am" collection: What does your child enjoy doing? What do you want to get better at? • Make an "I feel" collection: How does your child feel when you come home? When you go to Nana's? • Play a game: I say this when … I'm happy/sad/need help • Play a game: I do this when I'm upset/happy/sad …

Self-Management

Self-management is the ability to successfully regulate one's emotions, thoughts, and behaviors in varied situations—effectively managing stress, controlling impulses, and motivating oneself. It includes the ability to set and work toward personal and academic goals. Self-regulation has been found to be more predictive of school success than grades, standardized tests, or GPA because, according to Laurence Steinberg, "self-control is the main contributor to traits like perseverance, determination, and grit, all of which have been linked to higher school achievement as well as to success in the world of work," (*Educational Leadership,* 2015, p. 28).

Principal areas for support in a child's development of self-management

Self-management focuses on effective management of impulses and motivation. In addition, it addresses how a child manages stress. The proof of effective management comes when a child can achieve his or her personal and/or academic goals.

Questions you can ask yourself and your child (perhaps indirectly) to support the child's growth in self-management:

Recognizing management of emotions and their resultant behaviors

Y:　When you were angry at your brother, what did you do?

E:　When you and your group were called to the principal's office, how did you feel?

YA:　When Sheila felt afraid walking home, what did she do? What would you have done?

Understanding management of thoughts and their resultant behaviors

Y:　Did you think you were wrong? What did you do? Why?

E:　When Max was sent to bed without any supper, what did he do? Then what happened? Would you have done the same thing as Max? What are some of the problems that can come from being so wild?

YA:　What does "assume positive intent" mean? Does that apply to the way you go along with some of the comments made on social media? Who do you think misunderstands others or assumes negative intent of others? Is sarcasm a form of bullying?

Understanding how to manage stressful situations

Y: When you walked out of the room and yelled that the music is too loud, what were you thinking?

E: When you decided to leave the class, and just got up and went to the office, how did you feel? When you were called to the principal's office about leaving the class, how did you feel? What else might you have done?

YA: When you were late, and your phone battery ran out, what did you do? What else might you have done?

Understanding how to motivate yourself

Y: When it's time to get ready to leave for Nana's, what are the steps you're going to take?

E: What makes you feel unmotivated when you need to write? What do you feel? What do you think? How can you get started? How can you build stamina?

YA: When you must go to work, what do you do to get focused? What else might you do?

YA: Do you think "Fake it until you make it" might work to increase your motivation to talk at dinner time?

Understanding how to manage impulses

Y: What were you thinking when you took Tommy's baseball home? What are you thinking now? What should you do about this?

E: Tell me what you were thinking today when you got in trouble at school for throwing your book. Why did you throw the book?

YA: You said you felt anxious when you made the guys take you home. What were you thinking about? Was there some specific thing that happened?

Knowing how to accomplish personal and academic goals

Y: So, you setting a goal of getting dressed all by yourself. Will it help if you choose your clothes before we read your story at night? What else might help you do this? And, after you have gotten dressed by yourself for a week, should we celebrate by reading an extra story?

E: Your goal is to put your phone away during dinner. What steps do we need to take to make this happen?

YA: Your goal is to get all your job applications done on time. What do you need to do to get ready for an interview?

Activities that support deep, engaging discussions about self-management

Y: Keep a chart of a goal on the refrigerator or in your room.

Y: Play board games, outdoor games, or do a project with your family for at least one hour a day.

E: Set a goal. Keep a chart with post-its or markers. Figure out what you will do for yourself if you accomplish it.

E: Play board games, outdoor games, or do a project with your family for at least one hour a day.

YA: Set a goal for yourself that is meaningful, and keep track on a cell-phone app.

YA: Make time to be with your family for at least one hour a day while playing board games, outdoor games, or working on a family project.

Table 4.3 Summary of Self-Management Skills

Self-Management Skill	SEL Behaviors	SEL Activities
Self-management is the ability to successfully regulate one's emotions, thoughts, and behaviors in varied situations— effectively managing stress, controlling impulses, and motivating oneself. The skill includes the ability to set and work toward personal and academic goals.	● Impulse control ● Stress management ● Self-discipline ● Self-motivation ● Goal-setting ● Organizational skills	**Questions** ● What goal would you like to set? ● When you feel angry, what can you do so that you don't explode? ● How could we organize? **Activities** ● Read a shared book, blog, or magazine ● Create a selfie book ● How do you calm yourself? ● Stamina game for reading ● Stamina game for writing ● Stamina game for telling stories or singing ● Mindfulness breaks ● Brain breaks ● What did I say? Echo game ● How can I say this differently? (mean words, fresh words, angry words) ● He/she feels— I wonder how he/she feels when this happened?

Social-Awareness

Principal areas for support in a child's development in social-awareness

Empathy and perspective-taking

Y: How do you think Homer felt when Charlotte died?

E: When your sister's team lost, how do you think she felt?

YA: When friends bully others in social networks, why do they do it? How does it make the person they're targeting feel?

Diverse cultures and diverse people

Y: When we went to the Special Olympics, how did you feel?

E: One of your friends just moved here from Puerto Rico; do you think he feels lonely?

YA: When you read these multicultural books for your project, what did you discover about yourself, your friends, and your beliefs?

Social and ethical norms for behavior

Y: When Jimmy and Suzie had a fight, who broke the rules of the team?

E: When someone breaks a confidence, is that wrong?

YA: If you were sent a picture that might embarrass your friend, would you share it? With your friend? With others?

How to get support for concerns about family, school, and community

Y: If someone is bullying you on the team, who do you talk to?

E: If a family is in trouble because of addiction or alcoholism, who can you talk to?

YA: If you know that one of your friends stole money from her job, what would you do?

Activities that support deep, engaging discussions about social-awareness

Y: Read stories about diverse cultures and diverse people.

Y: Draw pictures about books you've read.

E: Draw a picture based on the books you've read about diverse cultures and diverse people. Include yourself in the picture.

E: Go to an event that celebrates a different culture and talk about what you see.

YA: Use social media or neighborhood events to discuss diversity. Tell family stories and discuss immigration, neighborhoods, and values.

Table 4.4 Summary of Social-Awareness Skills

Social-Awareness Skill	SEL Behaviors	SEL Activities
Social awareness is the ability to take the perspective of and to empathize with others, including those from diverse backgrounds and cultures. The skill includes the ability to understand social and ethical norms for behavior, and to recognize family, school, and community resources and support.	• Perspective-taking • Empathy • Appreciating diversity • Respect for others	**Questions** • How do you think he feels when …? • How might you make friends with …? **Activities** • Read a shared book, blog, or magazine • Random acts of kindness at home • Random acts of kindness in the neighborhood or with friends • Puppets • Growth mindset—charting goals • I want … • I can wait … • I am upset …

Relationship Skills

Principal areas for support in a child's development of relationship skills

Establishing and maintaining healthy relationships

> **Y:** What is a good friend?
>
> **E:** How do you choose your friends?
>
> **YA:** Why don't you talk to Jim anymore?

Establishing and maintaining healthy relationships with diverse individuals and groups

> **Y:** How do you get along with the kids on the T-ball team?
>
> **E:** Where will you volunteer for the church project?
>
> **YA:** You told me you met a new student from another country at school. Have you talked to her?

Collaborating and communicating effectively with others

> **Y:** How is your new T-ball team going?
>
> **E:** How is the youth group you joined going?
>
> **YA:** The LGBT group that you joined—how is it going?

Listening respectfully and attentively to others' ideas

> **Y:** What did the coach say today at T-ball?
>
> **E:** What happened today at youth group?
>
> **YA:** What is the new LGBT group saying at school?

Resisting social pressure

> **Y:** If someone makes fun of another person, what do you do?
>
> **E:** If you see a post on social media that is mean to someone, what do you do?
>
> **YA:** What do you do if someone is demeaning to another person?

Resolving conflict effectively

> **Y:** Tell me how you solved your problem about taking turns.
>
> **E:** How did you resolve your problem with Sandy's telling lies?
>
> **YA:** What happened when you met with your teacher about her giving you a demerit?

Offering support

Y: Jim seems to be sad these days. Want to ask him on a play date?

F: What did you say to Lindy when you learned she lost her Nana?

YA: Does your club offer support to students who are getting low grades?

Activities that support deep, engaging discussions about relationship skills

Y: Draw a picture of your friends.

Y: Tell me what you think of each of your friends.

E: Draw a picture about friendship.

E: Make up a story about good and bad friends.

YA: What are you doing for your service learning this year?

YA: How would you rank your friends, from most trustworthy to least trustworthy?

Table 4.5 Summary of Relationship Skills

Relationship Skills	SEL Behaviors	SEL Activities
Relationship skills are the ability to establish and maintain healthy and rewarding relationships with diverse individuals and groups. The skill includes the ability to communicate clearly, listen well, cooperate with others, resist inappropriate social pressure, negotiate conflicts constructively, and seek and offer help when needed.	• Communication • Social engagement • Relationship-building • Teamwork	**Questions** • How do people get along on the team? • Why do you think that happened? **Activities** • Read a shared book, blog, or magazine • Create a selfie book • When she/he does this, I want to ... • When she/he does this, I am going to ... • Playing board games and taking turns, winning, losing, then talking about it • This is how I'll say...

Responsible Decision-Making

Principal areas for support in a child's development of responsible decision-making

Making constructive choices considering ethics, safety and social norms

Y: What do you think the team leader should have done when Mickey brought a Ninja weapon to practice?

E: When you read *Lord of the Flies*, could you think of a better way to resolve their problems?

YA: After seeing the movie *13*, about suicide, what do you think the characters could have done to bring about a better ending?

Predicting whether the consequences of choices result in the well-being of yourself and others

Y: What do you think is going to happen because he didn't tell the truth?

E: How can we stop bullying on social media?

YA: How can students help stop the opioid crisis in the school?

Activities that support deep, engaging discussions about responsible decision-making

Y: Draw a picture of what you would do next.

Y: Tell a story about your solution. Does each person feel better with your solution?

E: Tell me how you'd solve the problems in the book or movie. Is everyone better off with your solution?

YA: Have any of your friends had problems like the one I just heard about from the neighbors?

Table 4.6 Summary of Responsible Decision-Making Skills

Decision-Making Skill	SEL Behaviors	SEL Activities
Responsible decision-making is the ability to make constructive choices about personal behavior and social interactions, based on ethical standards, safety concerns, and social norms. The skill includes the realistic evaluation of consequences of various actions, and a consideration of the well-being of oneself and others.	• Identifying problems • Analyzing situations • Solving problems • Evaluating • Reflecting • Ethical responsibility	**Questions** • How would you solve this problem? • Why isn't this a good plan? **Activities** • Read a shared book, blog, or magazine • What would you do if …? • Is this a solution that doesn't hurt anyone? • Is this ethical? • Why did you… Why didn't you …?

Parents and Guardians: Coaches for Life

The type of conversations that arise from probing questions and important topics are often consequential and serious. When you approach such a discussion, trying to assume a neutral stance and using the news, friends' stories, movies, and books can relieve some of the personal focus and take the stress out of the discussions.

As parent or guardian, sharing your wisdom and knowledge with your child is essential from his or her earliest years. Through questions, parents can help children see the patterns in their thinking and in their behaviors. I can still remember my mother saying (after stating her very clear opinion)—her words still resonate, "Do what you want, IT'S YOUR LIFE." I did have a choice, but as I made my choice, I knew the consequences.

When you develop and maintain a deep and abiding relationship and make time to talk, your child will always have a "safe space" in this sometimes dangerous and difficult world.

Resources

Classic Books with SEL Themes

All ages: *Where the Wild Things Are*, Sendak, M.—self-awareness, self-management

Y, E: *No, David!*, Shannon, D.—self-awareness, self-management, problem-solving

All: *The Giving Tree*, Silverstein, S.—social awareness, social relationships, problem-solving

Y, E: *Green Eggs and Ham*, Seuss—social awareness, social relationships, problem-solving

Y, E: *The Most Magnificent Thing*, Ashley Spires—all (Growth Mindset)

YA: *Wonder*, Raquel J. Palachio—social awareness, social relationships, problem-solving (diversity)

Classic Movies with SEL Themes

All ages: *Inside Out*

Y, E: *Babe*—social awareness, social relationships, problem-solving

All: *Up*—social awareness, social relationships, problem-solving , diversity (old age)

All: *Toy Story*—social awareness, social relationships, problem-solving

All: *Finding Nemo*—social awareness, social relationships, problem-solving

All: *The Lorax*—social awareness, social relationships, problem-solving

All: *Wall-E*—social awareness, social relationships, problem-solving

YA: *Freedom Writers*—social awareness, social relationships, problem-solving

YA: *Trainspotting*—social awareness, social relationships, problem-solving

YA: *Election*—social awareness, social relationships, problem-solving (gossip)

YA: *Bend It Like Beckham*—social awareness, social relationships, problem-solving (girls having power)

YA: *Mean Girls*—social awareness, social relationships, problem-solving (bullying)

YA: *Remembering the Titans*—social awareness, social relationships, problem-solving (race)

Classic Activities and SEL

Charting Goals—self-management, self-awareness

Journaling, Writing Stories, Making Books—all

Board Games—all types, for social awareness, social relationships, problem-solving

Drawing—all

Reading Out Loud—all

Online

Teach with Movies provides lists of quality movies and themes related to each movie. www.Teachwithmovies.com

Goodreads can provide lists of social-emotionally themed books for different ages. www.Goodreads.com

American Library Association *Booklists* provides lists of books that have been recognized as having high quality for children, middle-graders, young adults and adults https://www.booklistonline.com/

Association for Library Service to Children booklists, by grade level and theme, summer reading, gift books, notable children's books, etc. http://www.ala.org/alsc/publications-resources/book-lists

Online free books for English learners of all ages. http://larryferlazzo.edublogs.org/2011/11/21/a-collection-of-the-best-lists-for-online-books-accessible-to-ells/

The Web Site "What Do We Do All Day?" has over 200 lists of books called "The Greatest Book Lists for Kids," which is updated weekly. The lists include picture books, chapter books for early readers, elementary, and middle-level readers, poetry, folk tales, classics, read aloud recommendations, non-fiction, math and science books. https://www.whatdowedoallday.com/books-for-kids/

How to Talk So LITTLE Kids Will Listen: A Survival Guide to Life with Children Ages 2–7, by Joanna Faber and Julie King, with a Foreword by Adele Faber. *Publication date: January 10, 2017.* Scribner, an imprint of Simon & Schuster. http://howtotalksolittlekidswilllisten.com

Videos Stress Less: *Calming Strategies; Name it Tame it: Identifying Emotions, Building Social Skills, Tips to Support Decision-Making.*

http://www.parenttoolkit.com/social-and-emotional-development/video-series/supporting-social-and-emotional-development

Discussion Questions

1. Select a passage that resonates with you. How does it connect to your experience as a parent? Do you have examples of these connections?

2. What will you do to support your child's growth in self-awareness? List some books, movies, activities, and questions you can ask.

3. What will you do to support your child's growth in self-management? List some books, movies, activities, and questions you can ask.

4. What will you do to support your child's growth in social-awareness? List some books, movies, activities, and questions you can ask.

5. What will you do to support your child's growth in social relation-ships? List some books, movies, activities, and questions you can ask.

6. What will you do to support your child's growth in responsible decision-making? List some books, movies, activities, and questions you can ask.

7. How will you create a "safe space" for you and your child in which you can discuss social-emotional skills?

8. How have you established a trusting relationship with your child that is at the core of all deep conversations?

9. How will you encourage the higher-order thinking skills of reflection and metacognition? Why are reflection and metacognition so important to your child's development?

References

Beres, D. (2017). "How Reading Rewires Your Brain for More Intelligence and Empathy." http://bigthink.com/21st-century-spirituality/reading-rewires-your-brain-for-more-intelligence-and-empathy. Accessed September 12, 2017.

Gottschall, J. *The Storytelling Animal; How Stories Make Us Human.* Boston, Houghton Mifflin Harcourt, Boston, MA. 2012.

Kolari, J. *Connected Parenting: How to Raise a Great Kid.* Penguin Random House Canada, Toronto, Ontario. 2010.

Shechtman, Z. *Bibliotherapy.* The Springer Series on Human Exceptionality. 2009.

Steinberg, L. "How Self-Control Drives Student Achievement." *Educational Leadership* 73, 2, pp. 28–32, ASCD. 2015.

Widrich, L. (2012). *The Science of Storytelling: Why Telling a Story is the Most Powerful Way to Activate Our Brains.* https://lifehacker.com/5965703/the-science-of-storytelling-why-telling-a-story-is-the-most-powerful-way-to-activate-our-brains. Accessed September 12, 2017.

Zak, P. (2014). "Why Your Brain Loves Good Storytelling." https://hbr.org/2014/10/why-your-brain-loves-good-storytelling. *Harvard Business Review.*

5

The Brain and Learning

Objectives for This Chapter

At the conclusion of this chapter, the reader will be able to:

1. Explore the basics of brain anatomy and how the brain functions.
2. Explain the processes of memory creation and learning, and their connections with social-emotional learning (SEL) skills.
3. Use what we know about how the brain functions to support your child's development of SEL skills.
4. Use research-based knowledge of learning and memory processes to optimize your parenting practices in your child's acquisition of SEL skills.

In recent years, developments in the field of mind and brain education (MBE) have brought us to a new understanding of how learning happens in the brain. Today we have a growing body of research that tells us more specifically how learning occurs from neurobiological, developmental, and psychological perspectives. When armed with new knowledge about the brain, parents and guardians can begin to craft their parenting in ways that are more developmentally appropriate and neurologically sound. In other words, **with more technical knowledge about how the brain works, we can waste less time on ineffective practices and instead adopt empirically tested, evidence-based solutions that are more likely to yield success**. Imagine for a moment this typical scenario:

Mrs. Johnson, the parent of two adolescent children, has been struggling with one child to get him to clean his room and be more organized. Although both children have their own bedrooms, one child keeps an organized and very clean room. The other child has a hard time finding anything in his cluttered bedroom and does not seem to care. Try as she might, Mrs. Johnson is at a loss as to how to help. It seems nothing has worked.

The acquisition of basic and higher-order thinking skills involves a variety of brain regions that must be activated and allowed to communicate with each other via neural pathways.

Mrs. Johnson, like many parents and guardians, has not had the experience of considering the cognitive implications of parenting practices in developing social-emotional learning (SEL) skills with her own children. The brain is a complex organ, and because of its complexity, many people shy away from a deeper understanding of its processes. In this chapter, we aim to: provide you with a basic understanding of the brain and how it works; impart best practices for maximizing SEL skills with your children, informed by what we now know about the brain; and, finally, illuminate some of the implications of mind and brain education for your own parenting practices.

Through our own experiences as parents and guardian, we have found that gaining a deeper understanding of what "social-emotional learning" actually means and what precisely is happening in our children's brains when SEL is taking place are both crucial to using and benefiting from the strategies laid out in this book's other chapters.

Mind and brain education is a growing field. Over the past couple of decades, hundreds of books and articles have been published about the importance of brain-based education, brain-compatible classrooms, brain-compatible learning, and so on. What researchers have found is that the acquisition of basic and higher-order thinking skills involves a variety of brain regions that must be effectively activated and allowed to communicate with each other via developed neural pathways. This can be enhanced by adjusting our parenting practices to develop SEL skills in our own children and by taking account of neurological functioning. There is much to be gained from first knowing more about how the brain works.

Figure 5.1 The Brain

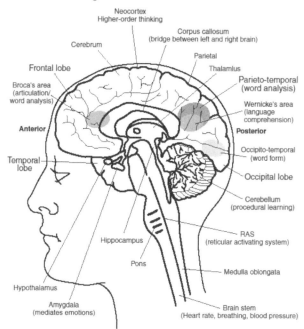

Brain Basics

The brain weighs approximately three pounds and is divided into two mirror-image hemispheres: the right and the left. The front of the brain is called the **anterior region**, and the back of the brain is called the **posterior region**. Each hemisphere is made up of four sections (also called **lobes**): frontal, parietal, temporal, and occipital. Together, these four lobes make up what is referred to as the **cerebral cortex**.

As you can see in Figure 5.1, the frontal lobe is in the anterior (front) section of the brain, the occipital lobe is in the posterior (back), and the parietal and temporal lobes lie between the two previously mentioned lobes. It is important to remember that, as the right and left hemispheres of the brain are mirror-images of each other, each hemisphere contains its own frontal, parietal, temporal, and occipital lobe. Table 5.1 further discusses the location and the functions of these brain areas.

What role does each of these brain sections play in learning and developing SEL skills in our own children? While the processes of learning and memory will be examined in more detail in the next section of this chapter, we can note here that the **frontal lobe** is used for higher-order thinking and fine motor skills, the **occipital lobe** for processing visual information, the **temporal lobe** for processing auditory information, and the **parietal lobe** for sensory information and spatial awareness.

The visual, auditory, and sensory information processed by the various sections of the brain comes from the body's five senses and reaches the various lobes of the brain through the spinal cord and brain stem (Figure 5.1). In addition to serving as a conveyor of sensory information, the **brain stem** controls the body's heart rate, blood pressure, and breathing. Behind the brain stem (and beneath the occipital lobe) is the **cerebellum**, which controls the body's motor coordination and motor learning.

Two other fundamental areas of the brain are **Broca's area** and **Wernicke's area**. Located in the frontal lobe and temporal lobes respectively (Figure 5.1), these two areas of the brain are named for the doctors who discovered that these regions work together to produce and understand speech. People who experience brain damage in Broca's area are able to understand the speech of others but cannot speak comprehensibly themselves. In contrast, people who experience brain damage in Wernicke's area are able to speak (and, in fact, blather uncontrollably), but cannot understand others' speech.

Located in the middle region of the brain (primarily in the temporal lobe) are the **hippocampus, thalamus, hypothalamus**, and **amygdala** (Figure 5.1). This area is sometimes referred to as the **limbic area** or the **limbic system**, and it controls body functions such as eating, drinking, sleeping, and processing emotions.

Finally, the brain's right and left hemispheres are primarily connected by a bundle of nerve fibers called the **corpus callosum** (Figure 5.1). Neuroscientists refer to the corpus callosum as the brain's "information superhighway" because it allows for communication between the two sides of the brain and for information collected in one hemisphere to be conveyed to the other. The corpus callosum is a key tool for allowing the brain to coordinate all of its different functions. In the 1960s, studies of people whose corpus callosum had been severed revealed that these people had difficulty performing certain tasks. For example, when subjects were blindfolded and an object such as a pencil was placed in their right hands, they could name and describe what they were holding. When the object was placed in their left hands, however, they were unable to name or describe the object they held. We will delve more deeply into the topic of left-brain versus right-brain functions later in this chapter.

Table 5.1 Parts of the Brain

Section	Location	Function
Frontal lobe	Anterior cerebral cortex (left and right hemispheres)	Complex thinking and using fingers to pick up small objects
Parietal lobe	Mid-cerebral cortex (left and right hemispheres)	Information coming through our senses, and awareness of space around us
Temporal lobe	Mid-cerebral cortex (left and right hemispheres)	Processing the information we hear
Occipital lobe	Posterior cerebral cortex (left and right hemispheres)	Processing the information we see
Brain stem	Base of brain	Controls heart rate, blood pressure, and breathing
Cerebellum	Base of brain, behind brain stem	Controls muscle coordination and motor learning
Broca's area	Frontal lobe	Produce speech
Wernicke's area	Temporal lobe	Understand speech
Limbic area	Temporal lobe	Controls eating, drinking, sleeping, and processing emotions
Corpus callosum	Beneath the cerebral cortex, and between left and right hemispheres	Allows communication between left and right hemispheres

The Brain and Learning

In order to explain what is actually happening in the brain when learning is taking place, we first need to give you one final lesson on the anatomy of the brain: all the different parts of the brain previously described are composed of brain cells known as **neurons**. There are approximately 100 billion neurons in the brain, each of which is made up of three parts: the cell body, the dendrites, and the axons. The cell body contains the neuron's DNA, while the axons and dendrites serve as "output fibers" and "input fibers," respectively. More specifically, a neuron's axons send information from the neuron to neighboring neurons, while the dendrites accept information from those neighboring neurons. The tiny space between two neurons is referred to as the synapse. When one neuron passes information through its axon across a synapse to the dendrites of another neuron, we say that the cells have "fired" across the synapse.

Learning is the result of the firing of cells across synapses

As you can see in Figure 5.2, one way to describe a neuron is by comparing it to a tree. The trunk of the tree represents a neuron's cell body. The tree's branches are analogous to a cell's dendrites, and the tree's roots represent the neuron's axons.

In short, learning is the result of the firing of cells across synapses. The reason that we become more skilled at doing a particular task if we practice it is that the neurons involved in that particular task actually improve at communicating with each other across their synapses. To have successfully learned something means that the neural pathways forged through practicing have strengthened so that firing can happen with little effort. Practice does make perfect.

For example, we learned in Chapter 1 that children travel through stages to master social and emotional skills, and these skills will likely have been committed to memory through sustained practice. While on the topic of learning, it is probably worth mentioning here that memorization does not wholly equate to learning; in real learning, people are "figuring things out" through logic, reason, and/or creativity. And, knowledge builds on knowledge: in figuring something out, we connect new ideas to what we already know.

Figure 5.2 How Neurons Grow

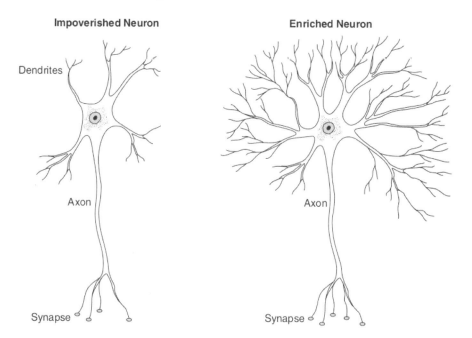

Example: Practice Makes Perfect

My husband and I liked to bring our daughter and son out for dinner on Fridays to our favorite restaurants in the area. Like many parents, we were always looking for an opportunity to get out of the house at the end of long work week and have some time together as a family. My husband and I worked different shifts, so being together as a family took some planning. I would pack a large bag of coloring books, crayons, children's books, little toys—anything that might keep the kids busy while we ordered and occasionally waited a long time for our meals. On one such occasion an elderly couple sitting across the aisle came over to us and commented, "How well-behaved your children are! Have they always been so well-behaved?" My children, of course, rolled their eyes furtively at me, since they privately knew that being "well-behaved" was not a trait they were born with.

To get them to this point, I used "time-outs" when they were toddlers and elementary-age children. If their behavior was loud, too active, too disruptive, or overall just not acceptable for a public restaurant, a time-out was called. I would remove them from the table and take one or the other, sometimes both, to a private space (often near the restrooms or outside) and quietly issue the time-out. We would discuss the behavior that was expected, how they could change their behavior, and how important it was to act politely in public because others were trying to enjoy a nice, quiet meal themselves. I found the amount of time and the immediacy for the time-out depended on the behavior, the restaurant, and how quickly each child understood what was expected.

The well-behaved children were not born this way. It took years of practice and many time-outs for my children to internalize the expected behaviors, and use those behaviors regardless of the restaurant. Sometimes, we cancelled the dinner altogether. My children figured out rather quickly—after many tries—that polite behavior was expected regardless of the restaurant. My children have since grown. To this day, they remember the time-outs and how polite and well-behaved they became in a restaurant! As parents we helped both children generate alternatives to counter-productive behavior and to respect others in the process.

Potentiation

This brings us to the concept of potentiation. As Barbara Given (2002) explains, "**Scientists have learned that neurons that fire frequently remain active.** This consistent state is called **potentiation**, which causes neurons to develop additional dendritic branches. Thus, [neurons] increase their ability to collect more information as learning occurs." To go back to the analogy of the neuron as a tree (Figure 5.2), when a young child is first taught a new word, such as "tree," synapses fire in the child's brain, connecting all the neurons necessary to process the new information. When a parent or guardian reads a book filled with illustrations of trees to their child, the dendrites of the particular neurons that process information about trees actually grow.

Potentiation can be applied to our parenting as we help develop SEL skills in our children. For example, in labeling and recognizing their own and others' emotions, children need multiple opportunities to process the information and practice this skill. The neurons in our children's brains continue to fire rapidly. If our adolescent storms into the house and announces that he or she had a terrible day at school—but doesn't want to talk about it, this might be the perfect moment to help our teenager identify his or her feelings *and* talk about it. The more we open doors for conversations that identify and discuss how the teen feels when issues arise, the greater the likelihood of his or her employing self-awareness skills in dealing with these issues. According to Goswami (2004), the average individual's brain quadruples in size between birth and adulthood. This increase in size is due primarily to the proliferation of connections, not the creation of new cells. An infant is born with nearly all of the neurons of an adult, but the baby's neural networks have not yet matured. As we will discuss in more detail later, the brain operates on a "use it or lose it" system. Individuals must continue learning and practicing in order to keep their neural pathways *and* keep them operating effectively and efficiently.

The brain operates on a "use it or lose it" system.

Neuroscientists sometimes compare the process of dendrites growing bushier to an athlete's muscles growing stronger when the athlete lifts weights. Just as an athlete who regularly activates his or her muscles by following an exercise regimen increases the strength of these muscles, neurons along a particular neural pathway become better at communicating the more that they are activated. The same holds true with helping children develop SEL skills. Parents and guardians can teach children effective ways to understand and appreciate other peoples' perspectives during conversations. The more that parents provide opportunities for important discussions with their children, the better everyone will become at communicating with one another.

A final point concerning brain basics relates to a fairly recent discovery about brain growth and adolescence. Prior to the late 1990s, the conventional wisdom was that no new neurons developed in the brain after a child reached between 18 months and 2 years of age. Earlier in this section, we mentioned that brain growth past infancy was largely due to the establishment of new neural connections and not to the birth of new cells. Research tells us, however, that there are some exceptions. According to Dr. Jay Giedd, a scientist with the National Institute of Mental Health, recent studies have revealed that some parts of the brain continue growing long after early childhood. For example, the cerebellum continues growing into a person's twenties. Moreover, the period of pre-adolescence directly before puberty and the period of adolescence itself represent times of significant growth for the brain's prefrontal cortex. As described earlier, the prefrontal cortex is the area of the brain in which the mechanics of thinking and emotion occur. For this reason, **it is particularly important that all children, especially adolescents, are exposed to a challenging school curriculum and engaging experi-**

ences inside and outside the home that push them to fully develop their cognitive skills in ways that engage both thinking and emotion. Equally as important are the opportunities we can take as parents and guardians when we create for our adolescents a safe, comfortable environment in which challenging conversations can take place.

Remember that, in the preceding paragraph, we compared the constant activation of neural pathways to an athlete's increasing his or her muscle mass by lifting weights. Unfortunately, the reverse analogy is true as well. Just as the muscles of an athlete who stops exercising will gradually lose strength and become weaker, a neural pathway that is not regularly activated through use will become slower and less efficient. As Giedd explains, the brain's system of "use it or lose it" means that neural pathways not receiving sufficient use may be rendered inactive. Thus, it is particularly important for children to participate in activities that activate as many neural pathways as possible in order to allow their brains to grow to their full potential. Then, like muscles, these neural pathways must be continually exercised so that the connections remain strong.

The Brain and Memory

Remembering a skill or concept means that neurons on its pathway fire so easily—communicate so effectively—that the brain easily recalls the particular skill or concept upon request.

It makes sense to follow up our discussion of learning with a discussion of memory. Broadly defined, **memory** is a recalled event that is elicited by refiring the neurons involved in the original experience. As Barbara Given (2002) explains, "There is no single storage area for records of the past. Memory is not a 'thing' but a process of neuronal network activation." In terms of learning and memory, the two processes are effectively the same. If learning a particular skill or concept results in the firing of neurons along a particular neural pathway, then *remembering* that skill or concept means that neurons along its pathway fire so easily—communicate so effectively with each other—that the brain easily recalls the particular skill or concept upon request. The same holds true in practicing SEL skills with our children. The more we identify, discuss and practice those skills with our children, the better.

Example: Thinking on Your Feet

A parent or guardian is teaching an adolescent how to handle a bully in one of her classes. Inside her adolescent brain, learning and knowing what to do if confronted with a bully involves activating a particular neural pathway inside the temporal lobe on the left side. As she thinks about bullies and engages in discussions with her parents about how to deal with them, the dendrites of the neurons along this pathway grow bushier, which allows them to communicate more quickly with each other. With enough practice, the neurons along the pathway become so efficient that the adolescent can quickly remember the strategies for dealing with bullies that she discussed with her parent. She becomes able to "think on her feet." This, of course, is the parent's/guardian's goal: for the teenager to remember the strategies well enough to instantly identify and utilize them if the bullying (or another negative situation) continues to occur.

While there is no single spot or system of neurons in the brain responsible for all memories, researchers have been able to determine the different locations in the brain in which various *types* of memories are stored. Eric Jensen (1998) explains that memories of sound are stored in the **auditory cortex**. The **hippocampus** stores memories related to speaking and reading, and the **amygdala** stores negative emotional events, such as an encounter with a bully. Memories of names, nouns, and pronouns are stored in the **temporal lobe**. Information regarding vital life functions is stored in the **brain stem**. The **cerebellum** is responsible for recalling basic muscle movements, such as pouring chemicals into a beaker.

Another expert in brain-based education, Marilee Sprenger (1999), illustrates the storing of memory in the brain in Table 5.2. Specific strategies for using each of the different kinds of our students' memories will be discussed later in this chapter.

Working Memory

Carter (2009) and Tokuhama-Espinosa (2011) recognize an additional type of memory, **working memory,** which holds special relevance to parenting practices. Working memory—one of the ways that the brain multitasks—is a system that is activated when one part of the frontal lobe holds a plan of action while simultaneously retrieving information from other parts of the brain. Tokuhama-Espinosa (2011) says, "Being able to

Table 5.2 Types of Memory

Type of Memory	Definition	Section of the Brain Where It Is Stored
Semantic memory	Information learned from words, such as the names of colors or the sounds of letters, taught to a toddler by his or her parent or guardian	Hippocampus (temporal lobe)
Episodic memory	Memory involving events and locations, such as a child remembering when his parent or guardian brought him to school on his first day, or going to grandma's for Thanksgiving dinner	Hippocampus (temporal lobe)
Procedural memory	Processes that the body does and remembers, such as learning how to walk, talk or ride a bike	Cerebellum
Automatic memory	The body's conditioned responses, such as using the color green to remember grass and red to remember an apple	Cerebellum
Emotional memory	Emotional information, such as an adolescent's excitement over an upcoming birthday party or anxiety about an appointment at the dentist	Amygdala

maintain information in one's mind long enough to perform a task is the definition of good working memory." When it comes to a good working memory, our adolescents are experts at pulling up old conversations to support an argument. The expression of "you told me last time that I could go" is a familiar phrase to many of us who have raised or are raising a teenager. Let's say that a teenager is having a discussion with a parent or guardian about getting permission to go to the movies with a group of friends. While listening to and processing his parent's or guardian's arguments, the teen might be simultaneously accessing his working memory to retain facts for a point he'd like to make during this conversation. While pulling up this information from his working memory may be an old strategy, the adolescent is also using the social-awareness skill of respecting a parent/guardian's point of view and perspective in the process.

So what, specifically, can parents and guardians do to maximize their children's use of working memory in developing social-emotional skills? For starters, it's important to note that working memory development occurs throughout childhood, but the most substantial growth happens in the first 10 years of life, with peak working-memory capacity reached at age 25. (By **capacity,** we mean the space of working memory, or the number of items one can hold in the working memory at a time.) This is an amount that varies depending on one's age. For example: The average 5-year-old can hold one item in mind (list of words, instructions, etc.), a 7-year-old can remember two items, a 10-year-old can remember three items, and a 14-year-old can remember four items.

Long-Term Memory

There is yet one more aspect of memory that warrants attention. In *Accessing the General Curriculum,* Victor Nolet and Margaret McLaughlin (2005) describe how long-term memory and new knowledge are linked:

> When something is stored in memory, it becomes part of a network in which various types of information (facts, propositions, concepts, and relationships) constitute "nodes." The more nodes and the more connections among nodes learners have, the better they will be at thinking, learning, recalling, and problem solving. … As [new] information from the environment is detected through one of the senses, it is held briefly until it can be analyzed. This analysis involves matching to the incoming stimulus with a recognizable pattern already stored in memory.

Information is more likely to become part of the brain's long-term memory if it can be connected to knowledge already held in long-term memory.

To put it simply, stimuli or information entering the brain is more likely to become part of the brain's long-term memory if that stimuli or information can be connected to knowledge *already held* in long-term memory. An adolescent who has already committed to long-term memory her parent's/guardian's expectation that she listen and participate during important conversations will subsequently find it much easier to remember those skills whenever important conversations with her parent/guardian take place. Why is this? Remember that, in cognitive terms, learning and memory both consist of laying down neural pathways through the firing of neurons across synapses. When someone can link new information to previously held knowledge, his or her brain is effectively linking the new information to neural pathways that have already been laid out. In contrast, new information unconnected to anything in a person's existing long-term memory necessitates the creation of a new neural pathway and the firing of synapses across neurons whose dendrites have not yet had the opportunity to become bushy, efficient communicators.

Neuro Myths

Left Brain vs. Right Brain

One of the first things that most of us learned about the brain is that the left hemisphere of the brain controls the right side of the body and vice versa. This is generally true; however, virtually every book written about the brain in the past decade goes to great pains to note that many misconceptions exist about the activities controlled by the brain's right and left hemispheres. Jensen (1998) writes, "While each side of the brain processes things quite differently, some earlier assumptions about the left and right brain are outdated."

Nonetheless, the right and left hemispheres of the brain do not operate identically. For example, Given (2002) reports that "the right side of the brain is associated with controlling negative emotions, whereas the left hemisphere is associated with positive emotions." At home, a young person's right hemisphere might be activated by disappointment at being told by a parent/guardian that he or she cannot invite some friends over for a sleepover on a long weekend. This same child's left hemisphere might be activated by pleasure when the parent/guardian offers that one night of the weekend for a sleepover is acceptable.

Moreover, the left hemisphere seems to play a primary role in producing and comprehending language, while the right hemisphere seems primarily responsible for processing visual, auditory, and spatial information. When, as parent or guardian, I help my child develop SEL skills, such as communicating effectively, I simultaneously tap into the primary role of my child's left hemisphere in producing and comprehending language. The clearer my conversation is with my child, the more likely the effectiveness of these conversations in resolving the often negative emotions when problems arise.

Sprenger (1999) explains that "the left hemisphere is able to analyze; it deals with parts. The right hemisphere deals with wholes. Analyzing music would occur in the left hemisphere and enjoying it in the right." In other words, a young adult just entering college might be asked by his or her parent or guardian which classes he or she enjoys the most, and how things are going in the first semester. The college student might use his or her left hemisphere to identify and think about each class individually, and then use his or her right hemisphere to identify the different emotions he or she feels about each class and the entire semester. The fact that we continue having important conversations about SEL skills with our children—even our college-age children—speaks volumes about our effective parenting practices.

In closing, there are some clear differences between the way in which the right and left hemispheres of the brain operate. Patricia Wolfe (2001), however, seems to best express the point made by various researchers that "although it now seems clear that our hemispheres each have their specialties … the responses of the two hemispheres are so closely connected that they produce a single view of the world, not two." Usha Goswami (2004) concurs: "There are massive cross-hemisphere connections in the normal brain," and "both the 'left brain' and 'right brain' are involved in all cognitive tasks." To return to the example of the parent/guardian who emphasized relationship management and communication skills when discussing a sleepover with his or her child: both hemispheres of the brain are necessary to carry out this conversation successfully. The right hemisphere allows the child to process the visual information in thinking about a weekend sleepover with friends, and then the left hemisphere allows the young person to find the language to put this visual information into words, thus communicating effectively with his or her parent or guardian.

Critical vs. Sensitive Learning Periods

Another myth about the brain is that there are certain critical periods during which the brain is receptive to specific types of information and, therefore, learning this kind of information can only occur during that critical period. An example that is often men-

It is important to distinguish between the myth of "critical periods" of learning and the reality of "sensitive" periods of learning.

tioned is that languages can only be learned fluently in early childhood.[1] While it is unquestionably true that early childhood represents an *optimal* period for language acquisition, during which children may acquire language skills with relative ease, it should also be noted that adolescents and adults are also capable of achieving fluency in new languages. Thus, it is important to distinguish between the myth of "critical periods" of learning and the reality of "sensitive" periods of learning.

Gender, Cognitive Science, and Schooling

As we move later into the 21st century, there are increasing concerns about boys' low academic achievement—worries that, in fact, boys are in crisis. Indeed, research does suggest that more girls than boys are graduating from high school, going on to college, and—for the first time in American history—outnumbering boys in our nation's law schools and medical schools. However, it is important to recognize that there is a cyclical nature to these concerns.

Cognitive scientist Daniel Willingham acknowledges that researchers have discovered some differences between male and female brains. On average, the region of the brain known as the hippocampus seems to be larger in the female brain than in the male brain. Males seem to have a slight advantage in certain spatial tasks and mathematical reasoning, while females seem to have an equally slight advantage in various memory tasks and mathematical calculation. Willingham (2006) explains, "Researchers

---

[1]   Early childhood is when children are less inhibited or self-conscious than older people with regard to trying and practicing the new language. This makes learning a new language easier for young children than for adolescents or adults.

who do this work debate whether these differences are very modest or moderate—but no researcher claims that they are large." This doesn't mean that there are *no* differences between male and female brains or that in the future neuroscience will not have more to contribute to our understanding of the differences in how boys and girls learn. Currently, however, **parents and guardians should be cautious about teaching boys and girls differently** due to the still-emerging science.

Multiple Intelligences Theory

In 1983, Howard Gardner published a work entitled *Frames of Mind: The Theory of Multiple Intelligences*. In this work, he laid out his **theory of multiple intelligences**—namely, that intelligence is better conceived of as a *multiple* rather than a *unitary* construct. Gardner argued that the traditional concept of intelligence is overly broad and that, in fact, different people are intelligent in different ways. This also holds true for our children. Gardner suggested that there were seven types of basic intelligences: linguistic, logical-mathematical, spatial, bodily-kinesthetic, musical, interpersonal, and intrapersonal (Table 5.3). In 1999, he added an eighth intelligence—naturalist intelligence.[2]

While Gardner's theory remains controversial in the psychology world, his theory of multiple intelligences is invaluable to parents and guardians because "multiple intelligence theory" reminds us that we should play to our children's strengths. As Laura Erlauer (2003) explains, "Success in learning is heightened when a student/child learns [via] his or her preferred learning style." Thus, when teaching SEL skills at home, it is beneficial to consider the child's preferred learning style, as found in one or more of the intelligences identified by Gardner. In a home focusing on teaching their young adolescent the social-emotional skill of impulse control, a parent or guardian might want to think about the child's preferred learning style. Below are some examples.

Have a conversation with your child to help create a plan for handling impulse control at home and school. Suppose you have an adolescent who flies off the handle, yells, and slams the bedroom door

---

[2]   In recent years, Gardner has also discussed—but not committed to—the idea of a ninth intelligence, *existential intelligence*, which deals with fundamental questions of existence, for example: *Why do we live? Why do we die? Where do we come from?*

Table 5.3 Howard Gardner's Multiple Intelligences

Linguistics	The ability to communicate effectively with words. This includes both speaking and understanding.
Logical-mathematical	The ability to develop solutions for and to solve problems. This includes problems that arise during conversations.
Spatial	The ability to recognize and interpret spatial images like maps, drawings, and paintings. This also includes awareness of personal and social space when talking to or standing next to someone.
Bodily-kinesthetic	The ability to use one's own body to create products or solve problems. This includes performing a dance, taking part in an athletic event, and role-playing to act out conversations.
Musical	The ability to produce, remember, and make meaning of different types of sound. This includes playing all types of music, rhythm, singing, interpreting a song, writing or composing music.
Interpersonal	The ability to recognize and understand other people's moods, desires, motivations, and intentions. This includes interpreting a person's mood, feelings, and attitude.
Intrapersonal	The ability to recognize and understand one's own moods, desires, motivations, and intentions.
Naturalist	The ability to recognize and understand the environment and to make connections to the outdoors. This includes taking nature hikes and studying natural phenomena.

whenever you ask if his or her homework is done. You were at a loss about what to do, but now have planned some questions that may get the conversation rolling.

Questions and ideas you can use in conversations about self-management with your adolescent:

- You said it bothers you when I ask if your homework is done. What can we do differently to help us both stay calm when it comes to homework reminders?

- What if you kept your assignments in your agenda and checked each one off as it's completed? How do you feel about that idea?

Do you have any other ideas that could work? (This uses linguistic intelligence.)

* Write or listen to a motivational song or rap that describes overcoming obstacles and working toward goals (musical intelligence). Talk with an older relative whose work involves self-discipline or self-motivation. Think about the adolescent who is not balancing school work with his obligation to arrive at work on time for his part-time job. The parent/guardian might suggest that the adolescent talk with an older cousin who is in a similar situation but is handling school and home obligations successfully.

Questions and ideas your adolescent can use to start a conversation about self-discipline and self-motivation with the older cousin:

* When it's time to get ready for your evening job, how do you get motivated after being at school all day?

* How do you balance school work with your job? Can you give me some examples? (This uses interpersonal intelligence.)

* Ask other young adolescents to reflect on how they manage and deal with personal or interpersonal stress.

Let's look at the following situation. An adolescent is from a home where English is a second language. He tells his best friend that he is embarrassed when he notices that his friends are having trouble understanding his mom when she speaks English. He doesn't want to hurt his mom's feelings, but doesn't know how to handle this situation.

Questions and ideas to help your adolescent have focused conversations with other adolescents about managing personal or interpersonal stress:

Notice in the following example how the teen (above) who speaks English as a second language talks with his best friend about his situation. His friend has some advice on how to manage personal stress. The conversation might sound something like this:

"When you and some of our friends came over my house the other day, my mom tried talking to everyone. I know she was trying to welcome everyone and be sure we all had something to eat, but I felt kind of embarrassed when she tried to speak English. I know you only speak English in your home, but what do you do if you ever feel embarrassed about someone in your family talking to your friends, or just saying too much?"

"This happens to me all the time, and my mom speaks English! I think your mom just wants to be friendly, but it also embarrasses me when my mom tries to be cool and overdoes it talking with my friends. Have you ever tried to sit down with your mom and tell her how you feel? Talk with her. Do you tell your mom you're really happy when she welcomes your friends into your home. Ask her if she can just say, 'Hello,' and welcome your friends in, and that you'll take it from there. Explain that you and your friends only get together once in awhile and not for long enough at each other's houses. I have to tell you, though, you might want to have this conversation with your mom ahead of time. This will give you a chance to really talk to her, let her know how you feel, and you won't be worried about hurting her feelings next time a bunch of friends come over." (This uses intrapersonal intelligence.)

Learning Systems Theory

Another theory through which to view the brain and learning is **learning systems theory,** espoused by researchers such as neurobiologist Robert Ornstein, psychiatrist Richard Restak, clinical psychologist Daniel Goleman, and education professor Barbara Given. As Given (2002) explains, "Current knowledge [of the brain and learning] … has moved beyond the left/right dichotomy to a broader view of five different learning systems—emotional, social, cognitive, physical, and reflective—and their numerous, often overlapping, subsystems that reflect specific neurobiological brain structures and functions." A short description of each learning system follows.

The Brain's Emotional Learning System

The limbic area of the brain (described earlier in this chapter) is the primary controller of a person's emotions. The emotional system determines likes, dislikes, goals, desires, and reactions to different interactions and occurrences. An adolescent's emotional system might be activated by receiving an upsetting report card grade in a particular subject, or a parent's or guardian's compliment about his or her excellent work in other subject areas. In both instances, the young person's emotional learning system is activated.

In Chapter 1, we defined the specific social-emotional learning (SEL) skills that make up each of the five areas of SEL. Some of those that are impacted by the brain's emotional learning system include:

- Labeling and recognizing your own and others' emotions
- Identifying what triggers your own emotions
  - Predicting others' feelings and reactions to your behaviors and to other situations—recognizing that the same behavior that you demonstrate might elicit different reactions from other people
  - Showing empathy
  - Evaluating others' emotional reactions to various situations

The Brain's Social Learning System

The social system of the brain controls social interactions and social emotions (romantic, maternal, friendly, etc.). It is perhaps the least understood of the five systems. Researchers believe that the right hemisphere may be more important than the left for social interactions and that the orbito-frontal cortex may play a primary role in determining one's social judgments.

Example: Let's look at the high school athlete whose social system kicks into gear whenever he takes care of two younger brothers after school. Sometimes, the teenager must miss his varsity soccer practice in order to watch his brothers. The coach understands his player's responsibilities at home, and works things out in terms of playing time. Back at home, just trying to make ends meet is a constant worry for the single parent/guardian who works a second job a few nights a week. One evening on the way out the door, the parent tells her oldest son that she doesn't know what she would do without his help watching his brothers. The son tells his mom that it's okay, because he knows that she is working for all of them. Someday, when he graduates from college, he will be able to help her more. "Besides, mom," he tells her, "this will give me good practice for when I'm a dad!"

SEL skills affected by the brain's social system include:

- Identifying verbal and non-verbal social cues (verbal, physical, voice intonation) to determine how others feel
- Predicting others' feelings and reactions to my behaviors and other situations, and recognizing that my behaviors may illicit different reactions from different people
- Showing empathy
- Evaluating others' emotional reactions to varied situations
- Respecting others (e.g., listening carefully, accurately, and objectively)
- Understanding others' points of view and perspectives
- Appreciating diversity (e.g., recognizing individual and group similarities and differences)
- Identifying and using the resources of family, school, and community when confronted with new or challenging tasks

The Brain's Cognitive Learning System

The cognitive system processes information received by the brain. The cognitive system exists throughout the neocortex—the four lobes of the brain. Each lobe is responsible for processing a different type of information: visual, auditory, sensory, higher order, etc. Whenever a young person receives information, the cognitive system is in full working mode. For example, suppose as a parent/guardian, I want to have a serious conversation about drinking and driving with my adolescent. I have been thinking for awhile about how to approach this discussion and I definitely want to have a two-way conversation. I am desperate to share information on drinking's negative effects on safety, well-being, and the ability to make clear decisions. But on the other hand, I do not want to turn off my adolescent.

The conversation might start something like this: "DJ, remember about a month ago you were *really* upset about someone who got into a bad car accident when he was drinking and driving with friends? I knew you were shaken up by that. At the time, I said we would talk about this together later. Now it's been awhile. Are you up for talking about it? Here's an article that I think you might want to read. It tells about what happens to the brain when we drink alcohol. Why don't you read the article? It will just take a couple of minutes. Let me know when you're done, and we can talk about it."

In this example, there are two points to remember:

1. Sharing information with an adolescent activates his or her cognitive system in the brain as the information is processed.

2. Conversations with young people are opportunities to teach and support them in developing their SEL skills. For more information on how to have effective conversations with your child about difficult topics, you may want to reread Chapter 3.

The Brain's Physical Learning System

The physical system draws information from a person's physical environment. It is situated primarily in the brain stem and cerebellum. The following example is one I can attest to personally.

Example: Let's take a look at a young adolescent who lives in a pretty rough neighborhood. Gangs are prevalent and trying to walk safely to and from school is a challenge. On this particular day, the boy is walking home. Squinting, he can just see that it looks like a gang is congregating on the corner. While gangs always hang out in this neighborhood, the adolescent is aware that if he keeps walking on the same side of the street, he will be directly in line with the path of this gang. His heart pounding, he looks back and quickly remembers a crosswalk that he passed a few minutes ago. He decides to retrace his steps and cross to the other side of the street at the crosswalk. In this instance, the adolescent's physical system is drawing information from his physical environment. This, in turn, helps him make a quick decision to use an alternate route to take him safely home.

The physical system draws information from a person's physical environment.

The Brain's Reflective Learning System

The reflective system controls the brain's higher-order thinking and problem-solving. This system takes the longest of the five learning systems to develop. It is primarily situated in the frontal lobe of the neocortex. The reflective system is activated when a parent or guardian helps an adolescent work on making responsible decisions, e.g., solving problems and reflecting on how choices we make now can affect the future.

Example: Let's say that an older teenager says to her parent or guardian: "Mom, I was thinking about something. Remember I went to Gina's house last week for that party? I felt really uncomfortable there. I texted you to pick me up early but I never told you why." She goes on to tell her mother that she assumed her friend's parents/guardians would be home during the party. When she got to her friend's house, there were a lot of kids, many of whom she did not know. It was pretty clear there were no parents/guardians or chaperones at the house. She tells her mom that there was a lot of alcohol for anyone who wanted it and most of the kids were drinking. She didn't want to make a big deal out of it, so she went into the bathroom and quietly texted her mom. While texting her mom, she remembered that her mother always told her, "I will pick you up anywhere, at any time, no questions asked."

While this story might sound familiar to some of us with adolescents at home, social-emotional conversation about situations like this are not always easy. As you may recall, in Chapter 3 there are procedures for resolving conflicts and having difficult conversations with adolescents. Also in that chapter, we explained how to prepare for important conversations with children, how to use effective praise and descriptive feedback, and ways to use stages in conversations with your child to resolve conflicts.

Imagine yourself in a situation similar to that which the adolescent above experienced at the party. The young person's text to her mom might look like this:

"Mom, I'm at that party. There's a lot of drinking going on and half the kids here aren't kids I know. Can u pick me up right away?"

The adolescent's mother grabs her keys, jumps in the car, and drives over to pick up her daughter. On the way home the mother doesn't say a word. As a matter of fact, neither talks. The next morning at breakfast, she tells her daughter, "You made a really good decision last night. I know it was hard for you to do, but you did the right thing. What made you decide to text me?"

"Mom, we've had tough conversations before. You always told me that you would pick me up at any time from anywhere with no questions asked. I kept thinking of how many times you have told me this. I guess it was the right thing to do."

While the five learning systems—emotional, social, cognitive, physical, and reflective—are described as separate entities, they are always working together. Let's think back to the earlier example of the boy who lives in a rough neighborhood and tries to avoid gang members as he walks home from school. All five of his learning systems were working together. When he saw the gang standing at the corner just ahead of him, he started to feel nervous. His *emotional learning system* was heightened. Quickly surveying his surroundings, his *physical learning system* kicked in. He knew that if he kept walking down the sidewalk, he would eventually run into the gang. He knew that these gang members were tough because he had seen them give trouble to other kids who walked the same route home. The adolescent's *social learning system* and his *reflective learning system* are working hard together in order to pull into place all this information. As he started to strategize about how he could avoid walking directly into the gang, his *cognitive learning system* was in full swing. He looked back at the crosswalk that would help him cross the street and thus avoid running into the gang. With all five learning systems in place, the young adolescent was able to keep walking safely to home.

What is the value of learning systems theory to parents and guardians? Given (2002) writes, "At any one moment, all systems simultaneously vie for attention and control." Research has revealed that the emotional, social, and physical learning systems all have the capability of overriding the more **academic** (e.g., planning, organizing, problem-solving, etc.) systems.

As parents and guardians, we need to be aware of and attend to our children's emotional, social, and physical learning systems.

For example, if a young person gets into an upsetting argument with her parent/guardian prior to leaving for school, her *cognitive learning system* will be unlikely to focus well on a math quiz at school that day. This is because her *emotional* and *social learning systems* are taking priority in her brain. Moreover, even if she does put the argument with her mother behind her, if she happened to miss breakfast she will be equally unlikely to focus well enough to successfully take the math quiz. In this case, her *physical learning system* takes priority over her *reflective learning system*.

In short, it seems that parents and guardians we need to be aware of and attend to children's emotional, social, and physical learning systems because of their impact upon youngsters' cognitive and reflective learning systems. If we sense that our child is likely to be distracted by some type of emotional or social issue, everyone will be better served by trying to talk *quietly* with the child before he or she heads off to school. We must have a plan in place for these occasions so our child knows that we can always talk and work to resolve issues together.

Strategies for Brain-Compatible Learning

Having spent the first half of this chapter describing different components of the brain, what learning and memory look like from a cognitive perspective, and the theories of multiple intelligences and learning systems, we turn now to the more practical matter of how we can use this information to inform our parenting. We have chosen to divide the remainder of this chapter into two sections: **structural strategies** for brain-compatible learning and **instructional strategies** for brain-compatible learning. In structural strategies, we will discuss structures and routines that are based on recent advances in our understanding of the brain and learning, which can be used at home to support our children in developing SEL skills. In instructional strategies, we will focus on strategies that apply new discoveries about the brain and SEL to our parenting practices.

Structural Strategies

The Brain and Prime Learning Periods

The work of neuroscientists has also given parents and guardians a deeper understanding how their adolescents' capacity for learning changes over time. According to research conducted in the late 1990s, the first 10 minutes of a conversation is when the potential for children's and adolescents' learning is highest. For example, the first 10 minutes of a conversation are prime time for an adolescent to focus on the point of a conversation he or she is having with a parent or guardian.

Imagine the following situation. A parent/guardian has been mulling over the idea of a conversation about substance abuse that he wants to have with his teenager. Ten minutes into the conversation, the parent/guardian is still talking about the importance of not taking drugs, but never really gets to the point. The adolescent starts to turn his attention to something else, like answering a text on his cell phone. To fully capitalize on the essential first 10 minutes, it is helpful for parents and guardians to plan ahead for important conversations (see Chapter 3).

Though the first 10 minutes of conversations represent the period during which young people are most likely to focus, comprehend, and commit information to long-term memory, a second prime period for learning occurs during the final 10–15 minutes of a conversation. For this reason structuring social-emotional conversations to allow a review of key ideas and topics at the end is valuable for ensuring that the discussion's content will become part of the young person's long-term memory. Recapping important points or strategies for handling various situations, such as respecting others, seeking help when needed, or managing personal stress, greatly increases the likelihood that the child or adolescent will understand and remember the content of those important conversations

The first 10 minutes of a conversation is when children's learning potential is highest.

If the opening and closing moments of SEL conversations with young people represent the times when their potential for learning is greatest, then it should be noted that the middle stage of conversations with adolescents typically represents their low point for learning. If I remind myself that such a low point exists, I can plan my conversations with my teenager in stages.

Example: Let's say I am discussing social-emotional skills for responsible decision-making with my adolescent. I have noticed that she is surrounding herself with (in my opinion) undesirable acquaintances. These friends stay out late on school nights, are disrespectful, and barely talk to me when I attempt to strike up a conversation during their visits to our house. Further, it appears to me they very likely have no supervision at home. Teenagers' worlds revolve around what their peers think of them, which means that having a conversation about choosing the right friends is challenging with this age group.

I might start our conversation like this: "I noticed that you have some new friends who come over and stay pretty late—too late when all of you have school the next day. I am going to ask you to think about how we can come up with a plan so that there is a limit to the amount of time they spend here. How do you think we can do this?"

There will likely be some push-back from my teenager, as she doesn't seem to think this is a problem. She may go on to say, "I can't just ask them to leave, mom. So, what do you want me to do?"

"How about we think about this together? I hear what you are saying. I know you can't just say, 'It's time for you to go home,' so what else could you say so they don't feel insulted?"

This conversation may take a few minutes, and we may find that not everything is resolved in the first stage. In this case, I can say, "Why don't you think about this for awhile? Check back with me in about twenty minutes, and let's see if we can figure it out together. Or, maybe you can come up with a good plan." As I offer both of us a break to think more about solving the problem, I am very aware of the low point that can arise in the middle of this type of conversation. Strategies such as "Let's take a break and think on it" help do a couple of things: they keep my own and my adolescent's emotions in check during a difficult conversation, and they help us both refocus our brains in a productive way as we approach the final stage of our conversation.

The low point of childrens' day occurs in the afternoon right after lunch.

Interestingly, children's high and low periods for learning in the course of the day follow a pattern similar to those of conversations. Young people tend to be the most alert during the first two hours and last two hours of the day. On the flip side, halfway between the time you wake up and the time you usually go to sleep is your low point in terms of energy and alertness. This finding suggests that the low point of children's and adolescents' day occurs in the afternoon right after lunch. Accordingly, parents and guardians might be well served by choosing to have conversations with their children in a way that includes physical movement (e.g., taking a walk; working together on chores, etc.) during their prime learning times.

The Brain and Technology

In the past 15–20 years, the Internet and mobile technologies have played an increasingly prominent role in all of our lives. With information readily at our fingertips, multiple online social networks, and the ability to connect person-to-person online in real time, direct conversations—like talking in person—are happening less and less. It is impossible not be concerned about the affects of increased exposure to technology on our brains. While there are numerous educational benefits provided by the

Internet, the implications of heavy reliance on technology cannot be ignored.

Technology brings about its own challenges for children and adolescents. As their use of personal technology increases, the number of face-to-face conversations they have with friends and family is decreasing. Further, technology has created a different venue in which children and adolescents deal with difficulties among their peers. The negative impact of public cyberbullying on children's and adolescents' self-esteem is clear. The question for parents and guardians is, what can we do about it?

Cyberbullying affects many young people, especially as they try to resolve interpersonal issues online. When a child is being bullied online, it is the perfect moment for their parent or guardian to initiate conversations that teach and solidify SEL skills.

Example: Timmy, who is ten years old, lives in a large urban community with his mom and sister. Like so many other kids in his neighborhood, Timmy, is bussed to a large elementary school that is far from where he lives. This school is actually in a "better" neighborhood than Timmy's own. Unbeknownst to Timmy, a couple of boys from school have been making negative comments online about his clothes and sneakers, which are mostly hand-me-downs from an older cousin. A close friend of Timmy's tells him that he'd better look online to see what the boys have posted about him. A shy youngster, Timmy goes home and checks online. He is extremely upset by what he reads, so much so that he tells his mother he doesn't want to go to school anymore. Once his mother understands why Timmy said this, she takes the situation very seriously and sees how destructive the online comments are to her son's self-esteem and sense of self-worth. She is aware that Timmy doesn't know how to deal with this, so she plans some questions before she starts her conversation with Timmy.

Here are questions Timmy's mother thought of asking:

- Timmy, when did you first hear that those boys were talking about you online?
- How did you feel when you first heard about it?
- How did you feel when you realized your best friend was nice enough to tell you about this?
- Do you know what this is called when someone writes something online that teases or makes fun of someone else?

- Timmy, what do you remember about the conversation I had with you and your sister just before you both started going to this school?

- We talked about how other kids can say mean things and we had some ideas of what you could do or say, What did you say to me then? What did you learn from our conversation about how to handle situations like this one?

- How can we plan together to deal with this [cyberbullying]? Shall we write our plan down?

- Who else do you think we should tell about what happened?

- Do you feel better now that we have a plan?

By planning her questions before starting the conversation about cyberbullying, Timmy's mother is able to organize her own thoughts first and then create a plan of action. In order to have a more focused conversation with Timmy, his mother recalls that the social-emotional skill of self-awareness is something she has been working on with Timmy for quite some time. Helping Timmy build the self-confidence to handle situations like bullying has been a focus of their conversations.

In this instance, Timmy's mom can help her son first think about past conversations they have had on how to deal with bullying. Taking it a step further this time, Timmy's mom can direct the conversation to cyberbullying and help her son develop an immediate plan of action that begins with "tell an adult right away." Since she planned her questions before the conversation begins, Timmy's mother is ready to talk with Timmy about cyberbullying and answer his questions. While cyberbullying is serious and may involve informing school and local authorities, Timmy's mom, through this initial conversation with Timmy, puts him more at ease. Timmy comes to understand that this problem of cyberbullying will be dealt with immediately.

The Brain and Nutrition

It can be difficult for a parent or guardian to influence children's eating habits, especially when they are not at home. However, it is very important to instill good eating habits early on, because nutrition—especially breakfast—has a considerable affect on the ability to learn. Neuroscientists have determined that what children eat (or do not eat) affects the functioning of their brains. As Barbara Given explains in *Teaching to the Brain's Natural Learning Systems* (2002), "It remains clear that children require sufficient intake of protein and complex carbohydrates to function effectively, mentally, and physically."

Thus, youngsters who arrive at school without having eaten breakfast start the day at a cognitive disadvantage compared with classmates who have eaten. An understanding of brain-based learning leads one to conclude that providing children with a good breakfast also supports their social-emotional learning. Adolescents are old enough to prepare their own breakfasts, yet they might choose not to or not allow enough time to eat it. Many of them may skip breakfast and/or lunch in the hope of staying in shape or being thin. In contrast, a young person who chooses to sit down and eat a good breakfast exhibits both self-awareness and self-management skills. While young people need food with protein and complex carbohydrates so their brains function effectively, there are other foods that negatively affect their brain's capacity for learning. As Given (2002) explains, "Simple sugars can be devastating to learning because they create a rapid increase in insulin and a 'sugar high' that is quickly followed by an overwhelming sense of sleepiness and foggy thinking." Unfortunately, the foods many young people eat for lunch are the sugary junk foods that lead directly to sleepiness and foggy thinking.

> *Youngsters who arrive at school without having eaten breakfast start the day at a cognitive disadvantage.*

Is this challenge completely out of our hands? Well, yes and no. While we certainly don't have complete control over our children's eating habits, the link between how children eat and how they think is clear. This means that parents and guardians need to take time to ensure that young people understand how essential good nutrition is to how well they can think—and to their overall well-being.

It is also valuable to remind *ourselves* about the importance of nutritious breakfasts and lunches. Much of what we now know about nutrition and learning has been discovered since we finished our own schooling. The importance of nutritious meals for alert, focused thinking can be conveyed in a respectful and helpful manner in meal-time conversations with our adolescents. Since all conversations can incorporate teaching and support for SEL skills, it makes sense that discussion of good nutrition is included.

Sometimes these conversations, especially with adolescents, do not go as smoothly as hoped. Having some social-emotional strategies ready for the conversation will help parents and guardians move closer to winning the battle on nutrition.

Example: A mother notices that her high-schooler is barely eating and is furtively checking her cell phone at the table. While there are two issues going on here, the one the mother wants to focus on is eating and nutrition.

"Honey, I noticed that you are not eating much when we sit down to dinner. Is something going on? Is everything okay?"

"Mom, I'm just texting my friend. Stop bugging me." At this point in the conversation, the teenager is already showing signs of shutting down, and the conversation has barely begun.

The mom goes on to say, "I am worried that you are losing weight. Can we talk about this after dinner?"

"I guess so."

While the issue here is clearly about healthy eating habits, the timing of this conversation is also important. If the parent or guardian in this example pushes the issue during dinner, then the discussion may dissolve into anger. What could have been a relaxing time together can quickly turn into a disrupted meal. If the parent/guardian informs her teenager that they will talk after dinner about the health issues that arise when we (any of us) skip meals, a likely argument is avoided as they agree to have this much-needed discussion after dinner.

The Brain and Sleep

Sleep is important for both body and the brain. As far as the brain is concerned, sleep plays a significant role in neurogenesis (the creation of new neurons) and in the system of converting information into long-term memory. Experts say that most young people need about nine hours of sleep each night but, unfortunately, insufficient sleep is a disturbing phenomenon that affects a growing number of children and adolescents. Many of them do not have regular bedtimes that would support their cognitive development, or their sleep may be interrupted for various reasons. For example, some youngsters stay up late watching television, playing video games, texting, or on social media with their cell phones. Naturally, when children and adolescents are sleep-deprived, the cognitive effects extend

Sleep plays a significant role in neurogenesis and in the system of converting information into long-term memory.

to their learning and their behavior in and out of the home. Negative consequences include difficulty with activities that enlist the prefrontal cortex (e.g., goal-setting, planning, decision-making), which is known to be sensitive to sleep. Higher-order thinking tasks, such as creativity and abstract reasoning, are also negatively affected.

Nationally, we seem to be moving toward becoming a sleepless society. A recent Gallup poll (2013) found that Americans currently average 6.8 hours of sleep per night, an hour less than the average in 1942. Sleepiness affects memory and attention, as well as general alertness. If it is becoming part of our national culture to sleep less, we, as parents and guardians, must emphasize the benefits of healthy sleep habits to our children. If you notice that your child is suffering the effects of too little or poor sleep, encourage a regular, early bedtime in an electronic-device-free sleeping environment to promote improved health and behavioral performance.

Emotional Wellness

In the section on "Learning Systems Theory," earlier in this chapter, we discussed the fact that when the brain's emotional learning system becomes distressed it may impair the ability of the brain's cognitive and reflective learning systems to function properly. For example, if an adolescent is concerned about an earlier interaction with a peer who bullies, he or she may be unable to focus on the day's lesson. This illustrates that **there is an important reason for us to pay attention to the social- and emotional-wellness of our young people; specifically, the state of these brain learning systems has a direct impact on our children's cognitive and reflective learning systems**.

While there is no need to repeat our discussion of those strategies here, it is important to point out that the interactions between the brain's different learning systems provide a cognitive rationale for investing the time necessary to create a home environment in which children and adolescents feel physically and emotionally safe. Such an environment is a prerequisite for maximizing positive social-emotional learning.

The Brain and Physical Activity

Among the many benefits of exercise on the brain, perhaps the most important has to do with oxygen. Exercise increases oxygen levels, so more reaches the brain. This has a direct correlation with improved cognition and task completion. Reflecting on the importance of oxygen to brain functioning, Sousa (2011) reports, "Higher concentrations of oxygen in the blood significantly enhance cognitive performance in healthy young adults. They are able to recall more words from a list and perform visual and spatial tasks faster. Moreover, their cognitive abilities vary directly with the amount of oxygen in the brain." The increased blood flow that accompanies exercise also benefits children's long-term memory, as the hippocampus functions more efficiently under these conditions. The brain-beneficial protein BDNF, which supports the health of neurons and promotes the generation of new ones, is optimized in the presence of increased hippocampal oxygen.

Adolescents need opportunities to expend energy and build physical activities into their lives. Therefore, we may want to consider ways of incorporating physical activity into our social-emotional interactions with them. We can stage our conversations during an enjoyable physical activity, which might make a difficult conversation flow more easily.

If we have access to a basketball court at a local park or down the street in back of a school, I, as parent or guardian, can shoot a few hoops with my child while simultaneously carrying on an important conversation. I cannot count the times I have done this with my own children during their teenage years. I found that they not only liked having me shoot hoops with them, but they also seemed more open to talking to me about friends and school than they would have if we were home. By pairing physical activity with good conversation, parents/guardians and their children begin to build a stronger understanding of and respect for one another.

Instructional Strategies

Practice, Practice

Whether we realize it or not, practicing when and how to have important conversations that build SEL skills is right in line with our own parenting and what science knows about brain-compatible learning. More specifically, repeated practice allows concepts, skills, and ideas to become more deeply ingrained in children's long-term memory, and more easily accessible through the increasing the speed with which synapses are firing along a particular neural pathway.

What kind of practice is most useful? In *Accessing the General Curriculum* (2000), Nolet and McLaughlin note that there are two different types of practice: *massed practice* and *distributed practice.* **Massed**

practice involves long sessions of intense practice at irregular intervals. **Distributed practice** refers to regularly scheduled practice sessions that may be shorter and less intense. In massed practice, there is significantly more practice at closely contiguous times than with distributed practice.

Massed practice can take place in social relationships, such as:

- Children are learning how to square dance.

- A family board game or card game could warrant massed practice in taking turns and playing fairly.

- Games like "Jenga" are great for encouraging risk-taking.

- Shared projects or hobbies can bring about massed practice in problem-solving, from making Valentines to repairing a car with Dad.

- Long car rides can precipitate repeated, massed lessons (for all the family) about patience and kindness ("She keeps looking at me and calling me a baby, Mom.").

- Family tragedies also bring about massed coping strategies, for example, during days of wakes and funerals.

Distributed practice refers to sessions that occur spontaneously and may be shorter and less intense than massed practice. While these examples do not at first glance appear to be related to parenting and conversations about developing SEL skills, they do support the types of practices that are needed in order for these important conversations to be successful.

For example, I am not sure how many times over the years I told my teenagers to be kind and to appreciate and accept all kinds of people. Possibly this is because I was brought up in a diverse neighborhood largely made up of different ethnicities, where most of us spoke another language before we learned English. I remember talking with my children when they were toddlers about how we should treat other people. I told them that each person is like a flower in a garden, very different than the next flower, yet a flower nonetheless. Even though I didn't know it at the time, I was using *distributive practice*. I never planned for when I would talk with my children on diversity; I just did it whenever the opportunity arose. To this day, my now adult children remind me of these conversations on accepting and appreciating the diversity of others.

The Brain and Making Work Enjoyable

When children enjoy activities and experiences, their brains release chemicals that increase their ability to remember what they are learning.

As parents and guardians, we want our youngsters to develop SEL skills in a positive and enjoyable manner. And, there is brain research suggesting that children and adolescents learn better when they enjoy their learning. Judy Willis (2007) says that recent neuroimaging studies have found increased levels of dopamine in people's brains during pleasurable and positive experiences. Willis explains why this is relevant: "Because dopamine is the chemical substance released at the end of a neuron associated with attention, memory, learning, and executive function, it follows that, when the brain releases dopamine in expectation of pleasurable experience, this dopamine will be available to increase the processing of new information." In other words, when children enjoy the activities and experiences in which they participate, their brains release chemicals that increase their ability to remember the content they are learning.

Some of the best conversations I've had with my own children happened when I least expected it. I think back to impromptu conversations that occurred around holidays when we were baking together. While no particular conversation stands out, baking actually became double the fun because my children were sharing time and conversations with me. While we were working on baking cookies and other goodies, our conversations focused on what was happening in their lives. Sometimes the topics were serious, such as finding out that a "best" friend was not really a best friend, and was actually kind of mean. Sometimes we talked about what it was like "in the old days" when I was growing up and facing similar situations. These times with my children were positive and memorable for all of us.

Reducing Stress

We live in a society that often glorifies individuals who can "rise to the occasion" and perform effectively during periods of great stress. While it is unquestionably important for people to learn how to *manage* stress, research on the brain suggests that high stress levels impede learning. According to Willis (2007), **during periods of stress, the amygdala—the area of the brain that regulates emotion—becomes so overactive that it blocks activity in other parts of the brain.** MRI results have found that individuals experiencing high stress show reduced activity in the higher cognitive centers of the brain. As a result, Willis explains, "New information coming through the sensory intake areas of the brain cannot pass as efficiently through the amygdala's effective filter to gain access to the brain's cognitive processing and memory storage areas." In short, placing young people in high-stress situations has been found to reduce the efficiency with which their brains can process and analyze new content. Clearly, there are situations in which stress is unavoidable; however, to the extent possible, we don't want our children learning in such conditions. Let's look at the following situation.

Example: A senior in high school tells her mom that she is already getting stressed out about final exams coming up the following week. She finds out that three of her exams are scheduled on one day and she doesn't know where to start. The teenager also works part time after school to help out the family. When she sits down to study, her mind goes blank. The more she thinks about how much she needs to study, the more anxious she gets, and the less she can focus on the material. Her mother thinks she may be able to help. The conversation goes something like this:

"Mom, I'm panicking about my finals. They're next week. Three are scheduled Friday, all in one day. Every time I sit down, it's like my brain shuts down and I can't think. I stare at my notes and start worrying about the next subject I have to study."

"Okay, honey. First of all, I know what you're going through. Three exams sounds like a lot in one day. I may be able to help, so let's try to figure out a plan together. Which of the subjects is going to take you the most time to study? How can we plan to give you a real break between each subject? How about taking a short run or working on your painting between each subject?"

"Mom, I'm more relaxed when I run. Maybe doing a short run between studying for one subject and the next would help."

"What else can you do to help you step away and relieve some of this study stress?"

"Well … we've been talking in health class about dealing with stress. Last week, the teacher had us practice things like deep breathing and stretching exercises. She even said reading a good book or imagining a quiet, peaceful place might help. Maybe one of these things would work."

Through helpful conversations like the one above, a parent or guardian can teach a child or adolescent how to deal with everyday stress without becoming overwhelmed. The brain is on overload when stressed and feels like it is shutting down. By giving the adolescent strategies such as mindfulness, deep-breathing, relaxing with a good book, or imagining a quiet, peaceful place, the parent/guardian hopes that the youngster will try these strategies on his or her own the next time a stressful situation occurs.

Using Different Types of Memory

You may recall from an earlier section of this chapter that brain-based education expert Marilee Sprenger breaks down the storing of memory in the brain into the following categories: semantic, episodic, procedural, automatic, and emotional. In *Learning and Memory The Brain in Action*, she suggests a number of specific strategies for effectively using the strengths of each type of memory.

Semantic Memory. Semantic memory helps us process ideas not drawn from personal experiences. Semantic memory includes things that are common knowledge, such as the names of colors, the capitals of countries, the sounds of letters, and other facts. In order to help a child use semantic memory, research suggests that parents and guardians can use summarizing, role-playing, conversations, outlining, timelines, paraphrasing, and mnemonic devices. These strategies involve adolescents' learning from written and spoken words. For example, paraphrasing asks adolescents to put information they have recently learned into their own words. Likewise, a mnemonic (i.e., a memory device) is a play on words that may help a child commit information to long-term memory. For example, science teachers help their students to remember the classification system of living things by using some variation of the phrase, "King Phillip Came Over For Great Spaghetti!" The first letter of each word in this mnemonic corresponds to the different levels of classification: kingdom, phylum, class, order, family, genus, and species. Such a phrase utilizes students' semantic memory to help them remember scientific information.

    Example: When it comes to having conversations with teenagers— perhaps about the dangers of drinking and driving, I, as parent or guardian, can use the strategy of paraphrasing so my adolescent is able to use his semantic memory. The conversation may sound something like this:
    "Joe, remember last week when we talked about how dangerous it is

to drink and drive? Did you read online about the car accident around the corner from us? Three kids from your high school were injured pretty badly."

"I heard about it when I went online yesterday, dad. It said that the driver's alcohol level was really high. The other kids in the car hadn't been drinking."

"What do you think happened? What would you do if you had no other way to get home than with a friend who had been drinking?"

"Dad, you've told me a million times that I can call you."

"Would you call me? What if your friends pressure you into driving with them?"

"I will just tell them, "No, I have a ride already.""

"Joe, I just want to be sure we are on the same page. Tell me, again, what you would say and do if you were ever pressured into driving with someone who you know had been drinking?"

The teenager paraphrases and says that he would call his dad right away to be picked up. He repeats that if any of his friends try to push him into taking a ride with someone who is drinking, he will practice what to say in his mind and then just tell them he already has a ride and doesn't need one.

Episodic Memory. Episodic memory occurs periodically—a memory of an event in a particular location. Memories of what we ate for breakfast, your first day of school and your son's wedding are examples of episodic memory. Researchers have discovered that *where an adolescent learns* a particular skill or concept and *where an adolescent is expected to apply this learning* may have an impact on his or her ability to recall and use this information. The context of where the learning took place helps remembering. For example, we know that children who learn something in one classroom and take a test on the material in another room consistently underperform.

Where a child learns something and where he or she needs to apply it can affect his or her ability to recall and use the information.

Episodic memory has an important component called "invisible information." The surroundings and events of the classroom become part of the context of the memory. Let's apply episodic memory to a conversation with my teenager. I want to talk to my daughter about the dangers and impact of smoking (or inhaling any substance) on the lungs and overall health. I decide to have this conversation while we are cleaning up the table after dinner. A few days later, she tells me that a girl who she thought she knew pretty well offered her a cigarette while they were heading out to go shopping. My daughter confides in me that she remembered how we talked about smoking a few days ago after dinner as we cleaned up the kitchen. This is an example of episodic memory. While the kitchen had no direct connection to smoking, the location of the kitchen brought up the memory of our recent conversation.

Procedural Memory. Procedural memory is responsible for knowing how to do things, also known as motor skills. A movement creates a "muscle memory" that leads a child or adolescent to associate the content they are learning with their movements at the time the learning is taking place. Procedural memories of parents and guardians might include early child care activities, such as feeding a child and comforting a child. However, after the first child, when everything seemed new and strange, when it comes to taking care of new babies, all members of the family benefit from the procedural memory of the parent/guardians. They know how to do it! When parents are teaching older children, procedural memory might involve playing catch or teaching the teenagers to drive. Procedural memory helps children remember what the body was doing, and creates muscle memory simultaneously.

Automatic Memory. Automatic memory is just that—information that can be recalled immediately without thinking about it. As elementary school students, most of us were expected to commit the multiplication tables to [automatic] memory. Automatic memory tends to require large amounts of practice, developing strong associations, familiar routines (e.g., riding a bike), or all of the above. In the following example notice how automatic memory helped my adolescent recall information immediately.

   Example: Whenever my teenager told me he was invited to a party at a friend's house, the hairs on my neck would stand on end. The discussion that followed must have happened a hundred times. Somehow, I thought that if I kept repeating the same message, it would eventually sink in. The conversation usually included the following questions: Whose house are you going to? Where is your friend's house? Will his parents be there? Who else is going to be there?

   In one particular conversation, I remember my teen saying to me,

"Mom, it's okay. I'm going over Jay's house. You know where he lives. His mom and his dad will be there.… I know. I know. If there is any drinking going on, you told me to call you and that you will pick me up. You've told me that if any kids show up that I don't know, to be careful. You *always* tell me to be aware of my surroundings and the people I am with. You've told me the same thing so many times that every time I go anywhere, I am starting to hear your voice in my head!" My child didn't understand that his automatic memory of our many past conversations was helping him recall details and information without even thinking about it. Further, he was unaware that this was my goal to begin with!

Emotional Memory. Perhaps the type of memory that parents and guardians make the least use of when talking with their children is emotional memory. Just as children are more likely to remember information that is connected to pictures, places, or their movements, young people are also better able to remember information linked with a particular emotion or feeling. How does this work?

    Example: Let's think about a really difficult conversation about bullying that a single parent or guardian had with his child. The teenager recalls how hard it was to tell his dad how bad he felt when his best friend was getting bullied on the playground—and how he had just stood there helplessly, doing nothing. While he grappled with his own stress over this situation, he also remembered how good he felt that he was at least able to vent his feelings and have this talk with his dad. He and his dad came up with some strategies, such as: tell an adult, or step up and say something. The adolescent's emotional memory, at first stressful when thinking about how he watched his friend get bullied, now shifted as they came up with a plan to act differently if this happened again.

Providing Structure

In previous sections of this chapter, we examined what learning and memory "look like" inside the brain. You will recall that adolescents are better able to transfer new information into long-term memory if they connect this new information to knowledge they already possess.

    For new information unconnected to previously held memory, one strategy we can use is **chunking**. This is the practice of grouping individual pieces of information into larger groups. For example, in *How the Brain Learns* (1995), David Sousa notes that it is difficult for adolescents to commit seven random numbers to memory, but adding a dash between the third and fourth digit turns those seven numbers into a "phone number." Since this grouping of numbers is more meaningful than seven random numbers in a line, these numbers are then more easily committed to long-term memory. Chunking works because the human brain is better at encoding information into long-term memory when it is received in an organized, categorized form rather than when it is simply individual, unconnected bits of information.

There are several strategies that parents and guardians can use to structure their children's learning. Chapter 3 described how parents and guardians might organize ideas by planning the "what" and "how" of an upcoming conversation on SEL skills. They can plan how conversations will begin; how to establish participation by the child; how to use appropriate praise and descriptive feedback; and how to follow up.

Example: Milestones—happy or traumatic—in a child's life sometimes call for a carefully planned conversation. Let's look at the example of a young adolescent, Kyle, who his going to his first dance. Kyle keeps asking his mom if he looks okay. However, inwardly, more is going on: he is very nervous about going to the dance. A few of his friends are going, but there will be many other kids whom he doesn't know. Added to all this, he really likes a girl who will be at the dance.

One hour before the dance, the Kyle approaches his mom and tells her that he isn't going to the dance. Thus, an urgent conversation using SEL skills starts to take place with his mom. Here's what the conversation might look like:

"Mom, I'm not going to the dance. I don't feel well."

"Kyle, a few minutes ago you were excited and telling me that your friends would all be there."

"I know, mom, but the thing is I'm really nervous about going. I don't know what's the matter with me all of a sudden. I won't know all the kids. What if I don't look good? What if some kids make fun of me? What if the girl I was telling you about doesn't talk to me?"

"Honey, remember, last week how we talked about self-confidence and feeling good about ourselves? You and I actually wrote down ideas on a piece of paper. You came up with most of the ideas. Do you remember what you wrote? Do you still have the paper?"

"Yeah. It's in my backpack. I'll get it, but I don't think it will help."

While Kyle looks for the paper, his mom scrambles to plan how the rest of this conversation will go in case Kyle's list doesn't do the trick. While thinking about how she has been talking to her teenager about SEL skills—self-awareness, self-worth, self-esteem, and self confidence—she formulates a plan.

Here is how the rest of the conversation goes. Pay attention to when the mom's backup plan shifts the conversation entirely.

"Mom, I can't find the list. It wouldn't work anyway. I do remember the list said that if I get nervous to take a few deep breaths and really concentrate on my breathing. Then, I have to breathe normally but still stay focused on those breaths. I'm supposed to think of a happy place while I am breathing."

"Kyle, you remembered most of the list. That's great! I want to tell you a story that I think you'll like. I know it's hard to believe but I actually know exactly what you're going through because I was your same age when I went to my first dance. I was incredibly nervous! I kept reminding myself, two or three of my friends will be there. They always have my back, and we usually have a great time together. Well, I went to the dance and mostly stayed with my friends. While we were talking and laughing, some other kids came up to us and asked if we wanted to dance together. It was really fun! Kyle, are there any ideas you get from my story that you can use tonight at the dance?"

"Gee, mom, I never thought about you being my age! That must have been a million years ago! Ha. Yeah, I get what you're saying. I actually thought of something, too. I'll do my deep breathing exercise right now. Then I'll picture myself having a great time. When I get to the dance, the first thing I'll do is find my friends. I know I can have a good time with just them. If the girl I like is there, I'll try to ask her to dance. If she doesn't want to, I still have my friends and other kids I can talk to and have fun with. Thanks, mom."

"Honey, when you come home from the dance, I want to hear all about it! Have a great time!"

When I have social-emotional talks like the one above with Kyle, I can see that many stages of a conversation often must take place. While one SEL skill may come from past conversations, there are other times when I have to think on my feet. In the above example, the mother quickly created her "plan B." As she shared her own story, she could see that her son was becoming less anxious. She was pleasantly surprised to see that her son had also been developing his own plan. By using examples and learning from memories and past conversations, they were able to resolve the problem together.

Three Types of Knowledge

Nolet and McLaughlin (2000) touch on a strategy for supporting children's learning. Parents and guardians may help their children employ more SEL strategies when they are clear about the *kind* of information they want their children to learn, and the manner in which they will be asked to use the information. The type of knowledge parents and guardians expect young people to learn may be divided into three categories: **declarative knowledge**, **procedural knowledge**, and **conditional knowledge** (see Table 5.4). Declarative knowledge takes the form of *known facts*. Procedural knowledge is *how to do something*. And conditional knowledge is knowing *when to apply* a skill or concept.

Procedural knowledge occurs as I model or show my children how to do something. For example, as parent or guardian, I teach my child how to welcome guests with some basic greetings, such as, "Hello, how are you?" or "I'm so glad to see you. May I take your coat?" We pretend that my child is the guest who rings the doorbell. When I open the door, I say, "Hello, how are you? I'm so glad to see you." My child sees and hears how to do something new—in this case, welcoming a guest.

Conditional knowledge is knowing if it is appropriate to use a concept or skill. For example, I may ask my child, "When will you use the skills we just practiced?" I am thus helping him/her embed the conditional knowledge as it is happening. To add to my child's wealth of conditional knowledge, I can ask if there are other social situations he or she is unsure about. We can discuss how to handle other situations, such as what to say if someone offers drugs or what to do if someone at school bullies him/her.

This is an effective means of teaching the relationship skills necessary in various social situations. Children often think that people naturally know what to do in social situations, but the reality is that most people *learn* how to act by observing others or through direct instruction from a parent or guardian.

Table 5.4 Types of Knowledge

Type of Knowledge	Definition	Example
Declarative knowledge	Knowledge of basic facts	A parent or guardian has taught his young child to say, "Hello, I am pleased to meet you" when greeting an new person. The child knows and can repeat these words.
Procedural knowledge	How to do something	The parent or guardian shows his or her child how to use the greeting, "Hello, I am pleased to meet you," when they practice this greeting together.
Conditional knowledge	Knowing when to apply a skill or concept	Child says, "Hello," and shakes the hand of a person he or she has never met before.

Using Color

In this section, we have discussed ways in which parents and guardians can organize the content they want to convey in important discussions with their children. Another strategy from the literature on brain-based strategies involves the use of color. In *Teaching with the Brain in Mind* (Jensen, 1998), the author suggests that parents and guardians may increase memory retention by using different colored markers to categorize information they write on paper or on wall charts.

Example: A parent/guardian has just finished a discussion with an adolescent about self-management and goal-setting in the specific skill area of *seeking help when needed*. This can encompass seeking help with homework, with getting along with peers at school, or even with doing chores at home. The child chooses to work on seeking help with homework. The two of them decide that a great idea would be to create a goal chart with a check-off list that can be posted on the refrigerator. Let's say they agree that the chart is a monthly calendar. The adolescent confides that the nights when he most needs help are when he has to study for a test. He writes down the days on which quizzes and tests are scheduled.

Then, he writes "NH" ("need help") in large letters on the nights when he thinks he will need help studying the material. Once they have done this, the youngster crosses off *NH* and replaces it with a star to show the work has been accomplished. At the end of the week, dad and child can see how many stars are on the chart. They can review what worked—and then consider something fun do together on the weekend. Figure 5.3 shows what the goal chart might look like.

Figure 5.3

December Study Chart NH = Need Help ⭐ = Done						
Sun	**Mon**	**Tue**	**Wed**	**Thu**	**Fri**	**Sat**
						1
2	3 *NH*	4 *Science Quiz* ⭐	5 *NH*	6 *NH*	7 *English Test*	8
9	10	11	12	13	14	15
16	17	18	19	20	21	22
23	24	25	26	27	28	29
30	31					

Conclusion

In this chapter, we endeavored to take advantage of recent advances in neuroscience to bring you a more thorough understanding of what is occurring in children's brains. We tried to balance explanations of how learning and memory occur with parenting strategies that incorporate SEL skills, as used by the writers of this book and recommended by doctors, psychologists, and scientists, based on their increasing understanding of the brain and learning.

We placed this chapter at the end of the book, recognizing that parents and guardians might view other chapters with a greater sense of immediacy than one that focuses on the brain and learning. We believe that rereading earlier chapters with a new understanding of the brain and SEL skills will help you during important discussions with your children. As more research on the brain and learning continues to be published, we authors have had the fascinating experience of more deeply understanding why and how *strategies that we have employed for years* actually work to support children's development of SEL skills. Deeper understanding has unquestionably increased our own effectiveness as parents/guardians. We hope that you, too, attain similar benefits from reading this book.

Discussion Questions

1. Select a passage from this chapter that resonates with you. How does the passage connect with your experiences? Give some examples of these experiences.

2. How will you provide structure in your conversations to support your children in developing SEL skills? Examples include labeling and recognizing your own and others' emotions, anticipating situations that lead to counter-productive behavior, predicting others' feelings and reactions to your own behavior, and demonstrating the capacity to make friends.

3. Choose an important conversation that you want to have with your child. Topics can include: effects of drugs and alcohol on health; drinking and driving; good choices when making friends; bullying, etc. Once you select a topic, choose one brain-compatible strategy (e.g., prime learning times; making conversations enjoyable, etc.) to use in the conversation with your child.

4. Share a time when you were young and learned something memorable in a conversation with an adult that has stayed with you throughout your life. Select a talk that had a long-term, positive impact, and that was embedded in your automatic memory. Describe choices you made as a result.

5. Choose a brain-based strategy from this chapter that was especially interesting to you and which you will commit to using during important conversations to support your adolescent in developing his or her SEL skills.

References

Carter, R. *The Human Brain Book*. London: DK Pub, 2009.

Erlauer, L. *The Brain-Compatible Classroom: Using What we Know about Learning to Improve Teaching*. Alexandria, VA ASCD, 2003.

Gardner, H. *Frames of Mind: The Theory of Multiple Intelligences*. New York: Basic Books, 1983.

Gardner, H. *Multiple Intelligences: New Horizons in Theory and Practice*. New York: Basic Books, 2006.

Given, B. *Teaching to the Brain's Natural Systems*. Alexandria, VA: ASCD, 2002.

Jensen, E.P. "A Fresh Look at Brain-Based Education." *The Phi Delta Kappan* 89, no. 6 (2008): 408–417. http://www.fasa.net/upload_documents/neuroplasticity10.29.pdf

Jensen, E. *Teaching with the Brain in Mind*. Alexandria, VA: ASCD, 1998.

Nolet, V. and McLaughlin, M. *Accessing the General Curriculum*. Thousand Oaks, CA: Corwin Press, 2005.

Ornstein, R. *The Right Mind: Making Sense of the Hemispheres*. New York: Harcourt Brace, 1997.

Sousa, D. *How the Brain Learns*. Reston, VA: National Association of Secondary School Principals, 1995.

Sousa, D. *How the Brain Learns*, 4th ed. Thousand Oaks, CA: Corwin Press, 2011.

Sprenger, M. *Learning & Memory: The Brain in Action*. Alexandria, VA: ASCD, 1999.

Spinks, S. "Inside the Teenage Brain," television series episode. *Frontline*. New York and Washington, DC: PBS, 1999.

Tokuhama-Espinosa, T. *Mind, Brain, and Education Science: A Comprehensive Guide to the New Brain-Based Teaching*. New York: W.W. Norton, 2011.

Willingham, D. "Ask the Cognitive Scientist: Brain-Based Learning More Fiction Than Fact." *American Educator* (Fall 2006): 1–9.

Willis, J. "The Gully in the Brain-Glitch Theory." *Educational Leadership* 65 (February 2007): 68–73.

Wolfe, P. *Brain Matters*. Alexandria, VA: ASCD, 2010.

INDEX